A Time to Mourn, A Time to Dance

Help for the Losses in Life

AID ASSOCIATION FOR LUTHERANS

4321 N. Ballard Road, Appleton, WI 54919-0001
www.aal.org • e-mail: aalmail@aal.org • (800) 225-5225

There is a time for everything,
  and a season for every activity under heaven:

a time to be born and a time to die,

a time to plant and a time to uproot,

a time to kill and a time to heal,

a time to tear down and a time to build,

a time to weep and a time to laugh,

a time to mourn and a time to dance,

a time to scatter stones and a time to gather them,

a time to embrace and a time to refrain,

a time to search and a time to give up,

a time to keep and a time to throw away,

a time to tear and a time to mend,

a time to be silent and a time to speak,

a time to love and a time to hate,

a time for war and a time for peace.

— ECCLESIASTES 3:1-8 NIV

Foreword

Life is a series of hellos and good-byes, of gains and losses. They come as a matched set. They are universal. Expecting to experience life without loss would be like trying to create a tapestry without thread.

A mom cannot say hello to a new baby until she says good-bye to pregnancy. A person cannot say hello to marriage without saying good-bye to single life. Young adults say good-bye to the world of school and hello to the world of employment. Every change or choice in our life includes some form of hello and good-bye— some form of loss along with a gain.

Often, we ignore those little losses. We neglect to recognize how, as a result of this continual succession of hellos and good-byes, our coping strategies are being built over time. It's as if life is providing us with training wheels to prepare us for the major losses that we are destined to experience.

In *A Time to Mourn, A Time to Dance*, we will explore those significant losses together. We'll look at the grief that comes with death, divorce, unemployment and other important losses that may impact your life. We'll look at how it feels and how it affects our lives and the lives of those around us. We'll search together to find meaning in grief. And we'll look at coping strategies that will help us lessen the pain and promote our healing.

You'll read accounts of grief—testimonials that have been combined from various sources. There are also resources suggested for when the journey seems too difficult to be traveled alone. Included are resources that can provide in-depth spiritual guidance and comfort— information not intended to be thoroughly covered in this book.

There is much here about the grief that accompanies death—the most universal of all losses. Please remember that a great deal of what is written can also apply to the many other losses that are discussed in this book. The feelings, the experiences, the expectations and the copings are similar in many respects.

A Time to Mourn, A Time to Dance is for anyone who wants to understand grief: grievers as well as persons who want to improve their ability to help those who are experiencing a loss.

We hope you enjoy *A Time to Mourn, A Time to Dance*...a benefit created exclusively for AAL members.

Special note to those who are grieving

The ability to concentrate is seriously impaired in grief. So be gentle with yourself. You don't have to read this book cover-to-cover. If all you can do is read a title, a quote or section at a time, that is enough. Feel free to skip sections. Find the ones that are pertinent to you today. Tomorrow, another section may hold the most meaning for you. In grief, it's important to remember that the healing takes time. Don't be impatient with yourself. Give yourself the gift of time. Healing cannot be rushed or forced by this book or any others.

Table of contents

Your journey through grief

No one is immune to loss and the resulting dynamics of grief. In this section, we'll look at those dynamics and what they can mean to you.

We'll define grief, look at ways to say good-bye, and identify the symptoms of grief. You'll also learn how long the grief process can last and ways to help make the journey easier.

Giving grief a name

Grief is an experience we all share. Yet, what is grief? How do we define it? What shape do we give to it? Grief is one of life's most poignant moments. Seldom do we talk about it, or try to find a definition for it until we are in the midst of it—a time filled with pain and confusion.

"Can my husband feel the same pain that I do in saying good-bye to our unborn child?"

"Can I ever hope to understand what it means to him to be out

looking for a job, after so many years with the same company?" "Will the children ever be able to understand why we got a divorce?"

Is it possible to find one definition of grief with so many variations on the theme? As uniquely different as the experience of grief can be, all grief shares some common themes. The hurt, the loss of identity, the disbelief, the physical, emotional and spiritual symptoms, as well as the time it takes to heal, are part of all grief.

Over the years, experts have tried to define those themes by using terms like "stages" or "tasks." Some may refer to the response toward grief as "adapting." Regard-less of the words that are used, theorists seem to agree that grief is a process, one that takes time and has no rules. Clearly, no one can grieve and find their life unchanged.

In this section, we'll look at the similarities of grief—whether grief is the result of a death, a job loss, a divorce or any other significant loss in life. Although death is the most frequently used example in this book, keep in mind that many of the symptoms and coping skills can apply to other losses as well. In Section II, we'll look at the unique qualities in different types of loss.

Who am I now?

As we go through life growing, learning and changing, we are constantly shifting and strengthening our personal definition. That's an expected part of life. It reflects a sense of control and purpose.

Grief, on the other hand, is a forced redefinition of self. It is a response to events that often seem out of control, without purpose, and frequently unexpected.

"I knew my parents would die someday, but not today. Everyone is turning to me, the eldest, asking me what to do now. What do I say? I'm not ready to be the senior member of the family. As crazy as it sounds, at 45 I still feel like I've just been orphaned."

Grief is the process of redefinition. Everyone's story is different, everyone's circumstance is their own. Yet with grief the resounding question is always, "Who am I now?"

❖ Am I still the mother of four or only three after my beloved child has died?

❖ He lies there, not even knowing me, totally dependent, trapped in life—not yet freed by death. Who is he now? Who am I? Daughter? Nurse? Caregiver?

❖ I don't even know where to tell people I live any more. It used to be simple before the divorce, 610 Maple. Now I have two houses. My parents even have two different names. So who does that make me?

❖ What is my proper title now? Husband? Mate? Or do I have to say widower, now that she is gone?

❖ Am I still a sister now that my only brother is dead? Or am I now an only child?

❖ I've always had pride in my job, my accomplishments. Thirty-five years with the same company before they closed this week. What do I do now? Who is going to hire a 55-year-old man? How am I going to support my family? Who am I now?

All of these are different circumstances, yet in all of them you hear the same question. Finding the answer to that question is the process of grief and the process of healing.

> I am bowed down and brought very low. All day long I go about mourning ... Come quickly and help me, O Lord my Savior.
>
> Psalm 38: 6, 22

How am I supposed to say good-bye?

Saying good-bye is often one of the difficult parts of grieving. Yet the way we say good-bye can also be one of the helpful parts of healing. Rituals of good-bye vary from family to family, parish to parish, church to church, and faith to faith. The details of designing a ritual can even be a good way to cope with early grief. One of the most important parts of a good-bye ritual is finding a comfortable way privately or publicly to symbolize our love, commemorate life and make a commitment to the future.

Funerals

Throughout history, most cultures have provided ways to make public statements of good-byes. If it is a death, the traditional ritual in most Judeo-Christian cultures is a funeral. The funeral acts as a way to recognize the death, express faith and hope in the resurrection, and celebrate the life of the person who has died.

Some churches allow the ritual to be individualized and encourage family members to participate in making the process personal. In those situations, all members of a family should be given the opportunity to participate in whatever way would feel comfortable to them, including the children.

There are many ways of making rituals personal, including special Scripture quotes, music, special poetry, flowers and sharing of special memories.

A frequently asked question about funerals is, "How old should children be before attending a funeral?" Currently, experts seem to be in agreement that children of all ages should be given the opportunity to participate in whatever way they feel comfortable. That may mean something as simple as making a card to put in the casket, but not attending the funeral. Or it may mean attending the funeral and even sharing favorite memories.

The caution about children at funerals is that they *must* be prepared by being told exactly what to expect. We also need to remember that young children have very concrete minds. That means some words or phrases that may seem comforting to you as an adult may seem confusing—even frightening—to a child.

For example, imagine how confused a young child might feel being told, "We lost grandma today"—yet no one is looking for her—and then seeing her in the casket.

Think of the images a child could conjure up when hearing phrases like, "Only the good die young," or "The angels came and got her in her sleep," or "God took him."

Later in this book, we'll discuss some of the things to say in talking to children about loss. For now, remember there is a physical and a spiritual reality about death. Children need explanations and reassurances about both.

Other good-byes

Rituals of good-bye need not be restricted only to a death rite. It is also possible to have a ritual for moving, divorce, changing jobs, etc. For example:

To help cope with moving, you might:

❖ Invite family members to write a brief description about their most vivid memory about your home. They can even include photos and sketches. Then, make copies for each member.

To recognize a divorce, you might:

❖ Symbolically, in front of family and friends, return the rings that represented the marriage, or blow out a marriage candle.

To recognize the death of a pet, you might:

❖ Gather the family together and plant a tree in remembrance.

To help deal with the empty nest syndrome, you might consider:

❖ Becoming a student of your children's career interests, opportunities and challenges. It's a way to continue meaningful communication.

A good-bye ritual can be applied to any loss. It can serve as a real, live, three-dimensional way to help you reach closure on your loss.

I did not know how hard it would be to say good-bye.

Yet it was harder still, when I refused to say it.

— A grieving widow

The "stupid things" that people say

I couldn't believe it. What was I supposed to do when she proceeded to tell me how busy her holiday season had been? She told me all the things she did, all the things she had to get fixed, all the cooking she had to do, all the errands she had to run. Then she opened her mouth, looked me straight in the eye and said, "Then your husband got murdered." It was as if she wanted me to apologize to her for disrupting her party plans because my husband was murdered a few days before New Year's Eve. I know she didn't mean it that way, but you can imagine how much those words hurt. And she was my friend.

When you are grieving, it's important to know that many times people may say things that hurt. It's even more important to know that it is not intentional. Sometimes, just knowing that others don't understand takes some of the sting out of it.

We've all heard stupid things. We've probably all said them. Like the person who said to a bereaved parent of an adopted child, *"Well, I know it hurts, but it's not like he was yours."*

Our friends, family, co-workers don't say stupid things to hurt us. They, like us, are searching for the right words, the answer, the "rule book" that will make this easier.

The only thing we can do is to be prepared for them. If we know in advance that people are going to have a hard time and say things that aren't helpful and may even be hurtful to us, maybe it will make it easier.

No, you're not "crazy;" the symptoms of grief

I thought nothing could be worse than the pain I experienced when my mom died. Who would have thought the pain of divorce would be as bad, if not worse. I feel out of touch with my life. One minute I'm thinking about all the things that went wrong and how bad it was. The next minute I'm dreaming about how wonderful it would be if we could start over. I didn't realize how much I identified myself as "Mrs." in addition to being a mom. It's been months now and I still have trouble concentrating on anything. One minute I'm angry, yelling, sometimes even yelling at God. The next minute I'm crying. I'm tired but I can't sleep. I'm hungry, but I can't eat. I worry about the kids. I wonder if I'll ever find someone else. It's crazy, isn't it? I should be happy. I wanted the divorce, but I feel so sad. Tell me, am I crazy?

No, this woman is not "crazy." What she is experiencing is grief. Grief manifests itself in many ways and it's not always about the primary loss. This woman's pain is not just about the divorce, but all the secondary losses created by the divorce: the change in identity, security, her children's happiness, the fact that it feels like it will go on forever.

The feeling of "being crazy" may be because she feels she is not living up to her expectations of where she thinks she "should be" in her grief. We must be careful about the "shoulds" of grief. **Grief has no rules. Not everyone will respond the same way.**

We often have unrealistic expectations for ourselves when we grieve. We don't recognize that changes can affect our:

❖ Emotions
❖ Physical sensations
❖ Thought patterns
❖ Behaviors, including social behaviors
❖ Spirituality

Emotional changes

Grief can include feelings of shock, numbness and disbelief. There may be tears that don't want to stop and seem to go on forever. Many people say life takes on an unreal quality, almost like a fog has descended. Anger, irritability and a sense of helplessness often accompany sadness and depression. Mood swings are common. You may feel anxious, fearful, lonely, vulnerable—even crazy. At times, there are even feelings of relief and then guilt for being relieved. All emotions are experienced with increased intensity.

Physical sensations

We can all relate to these symptoms, even though we may not be able to fully understand them. Grief symptoms that are part of our body's basic instinct for survival are called "fight or flight." When

> There is a sacredness in tears. They are not the mark of weakness, but of power. They speak more eloquently than 10,000 tongues. They are the messengers of overwhelming grief, of deep contrition and of unspeakable love.
>
> — Washington Irving

we are stressed, our nervous system automatically produces chemicals. One is called adrenaline. The release of this chemical and others in our body causes the feeling of breathlessness with frequent sighing. Other sensations include tightness in the chest, increased heart rate, palpitations, cold clammy hands, dry mouth and headaches.

As the stress of grief continues, our bodies try to adapt by releasing even more chemicals. The release of these chemicals (ACTH, aldosterone, cortisol and thyroxin) help explain a rise in blood pressure, shortness of breath, feelings of dizziness, changes in appetite, nausea, feelings of anxiousness or excitability.

Other symptoms, including fatigue, lack of energy and lack of motivation, can also be biochemically based. There are also changes in our immune system which leave us more susceptible to infections or diseases.

These symptoms are all based on the fact that our body is trying to react and respond to a painful situation. We can do things to try and help our body, but to try to stop the reaction would be like eating a sandwich and telling your stomach not to digest it.

Thought pattern disturbances

In grief, expect an inability to concentrate—to be forgetful. We may be in the middle of a task and not know how to end it. We may start a sentence and not know how to complete it. Time gets away from us. What seemed like only yesterday may have actually been a week ago. We plan something for next week and before we know it, we've missed it because we thought it was yet another week away.

Many people even talk about hearing the one who is gone, or walking into a room and smelling their perfume. Others may wait for the phone to ring, forgetting that the person is not going to call. There is often a preoccupation with the loss, sometimes even thoughts of self destruction in order to be with the loved one.

Behavioral changes

These changes can cover a full range of extremes. Some people can't sleep; others sleep all the time. Some visit places that hold reminders; others avoid them. There may be a need for social contact; or a need to be alone. Some people want to be held and hugged; others are hyper-sensitive to touch. Some want to gather together all the treasures of their life, pictures, memorabilia, etc. Others choose to close the door on the past, removing photos and discarding all belongings. There are no "rights" and "wrongs" here. These are personal choices, not ones to be pushed on us by a well-meaning friend or caregiver.

Many bereaved also point out that the behaviors of the people around them also change. People don't know what to say. They want to help but don't know how. They may try to over-control in an attempt to be helpful. Often they may withdraw out of their own sense of helplessness. Or, they may become impatient with your actions because the grieving "has been long enough" (in their estimation).

Spiritual changes

Spirituality at a time of loss can be the source of great comfort. God becomes a foundation of strength for some. They turn to their faith for consolation. Some people even find God through loss. For others, spiritual beliefs can be a target of anger. They may use God as the One to blame. *How could He let this happen? It's not fair.* Especially following a sudden or traumatic loss, many people find their faith being severely tested.

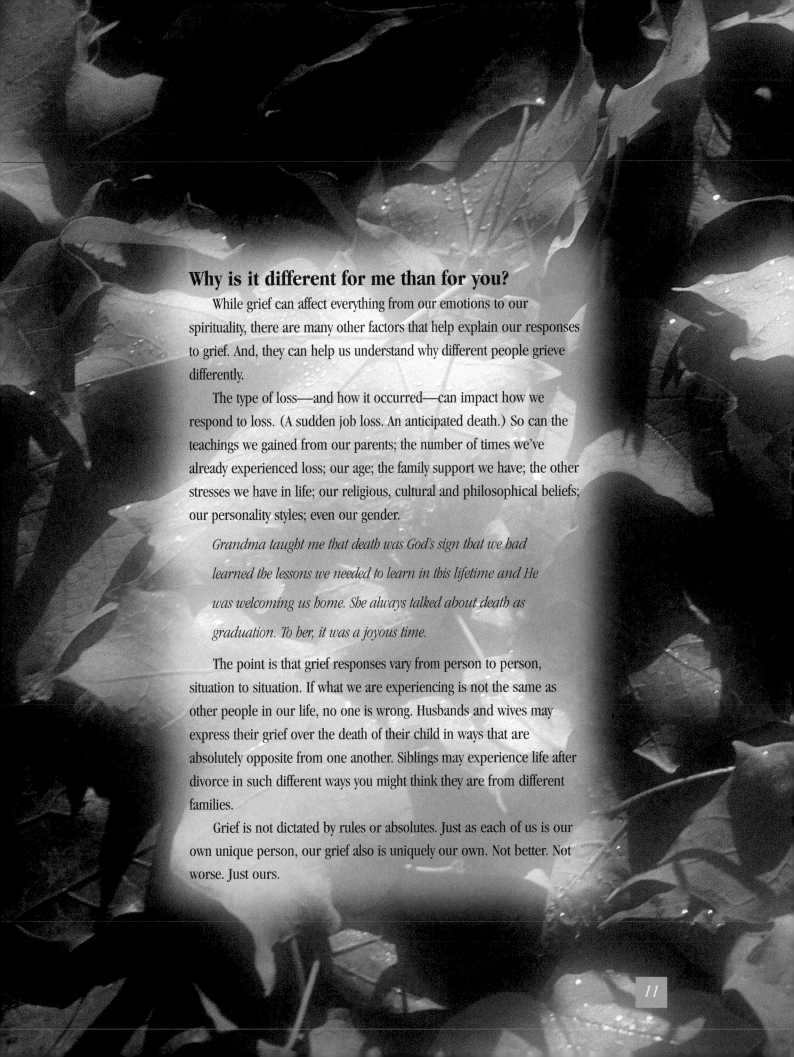

Why is it different for me than for you?

While grief can affect everything from our emotions to our spirituality, there are many other factors that help explain our responses to grief. And, they can help us understand why different people grieve differently.

The type of loss—and how it occurred—can impact how we respond to loss. (A sudden job loss. An anticipated death.) So can the teachings we gained from our parents; the number of times we've already experienced loss; our age; the family support we have; the other stresses we have in life; our religious, cultural and philosophical beliefs; our personality styles; even our gender.

Grandma taught me that death was God's sign that we had learned the lessons we needed to learn in this lifetime and He was welcoming us home. She always talked about death as graduation. To her, it was a joyous time.

The point is that grief responses vary from person to person, situation to situation. If what we are experiencing is not the same as other people in our life, no one is wrong. Husbands and wives may express their grief over the death of their child in ways that are absolutely opposite from one another. Siblings may experience life after divorce in such different ways you might think they are from different families.

Grief is not dictated by rules or absolutes. Just as each of us is our own unique person, our grief also is uniquely our own. Not better. Not worse. Just ours.

How long will it last?

Tell me, does grief go on forever? Or does it eventually go away? Someone once told me that it took a year. I waited a year. I counted the days. I knew that on day 366 the sun was going to shine again. The pain would be gone and I could get on with living. Well, day 366 came and it was a rainy, nasty, horrible day both inside and outside. The pain wasn't gone. In fact, that day almost felt worse. It took much longer before the sun shone again, but those first 365 days taught me I could survive.

We want to believe there is some quick and easy cure for grief. After all, we live in a microwave society. If we don't have time to cook, we slide something in the microwave, wait a few minutes, and dinner is served.

So how long do we have to wait until the pain of grief goes away? Ten days, two weeks, six months, a year? Wouldn't it be nice if we could find a way to microwave grief away? It doesn't work that way.

Quite simply, **grief takes as long as it takes.**

I always wondered if God's gift to us following a major trauma is to make us so numb that we can walk through the paces, deal with the funeral, take care of the things that need to be done, yet feel so little.

Numbness is a gift, but as the numbness wears off—usually six to eight weeks after the loss—we really begin feeling the depth of the pain and the loneliness. The irony is by that time, most of our friends have gone back to their own routine. It is then when we begin searching for the next yard mark of hope.

The first year—a year of "firsts"

The difficult part of the first year is finding ways to survive each of the "firsts." It takes a full year to get through all of them. The first birthday, the first Christmas, the first anniversary without them. The first Fourth of July, the first Labor Day, the first Thanksgiving. Again and again we are faced with yet another first. Maybe that's one of the reasons the first year is so very hard. But the second year is hard, too; not as hard, but the pain doesn't vanish on day 366. It's almost as if you have to get through that first year of the acute pain before the true healing can begin.

Anniversaries

Coping gets easier in the years to follow. Healing becomes more about learning to incorporate the grief into our lives. Life begins to return to a new "normal." It's like having a physical wound, a cut that will heal but will always leave a scar.

Many people say the scar again becomes painful and visible around the anniversary time. Don't be surprised by anniversary reactions. Like the initial grief response, they can vary in experience and intensity from one person to another. There may be just a sense of sadness, tearfulness or irritability. Or, there may be a brief but intense reliving of the trauma.

Whatever it is, honor the experience. Be gentle with yourself. You may feel like you're losing it or ashamed. Remember, anyone who has experienced a major loss has been there. Sometimes it helps to plan ahead. You might want to ask your faith community to remember the anniversary in prayer, including petitions for your personal strength.

You might want to spend the anniversary with family and friends. Or, you may choose to spend it alone. Plan something special for yourself that day in commemoration.

So with you: Now is
your time of grief,
but I will see you again
and you will rejoice,
and no one will take
away your joy.
— John 16:22 NIV

13

How can I find relief?

Some people see the process of grief and healing as a journey through a gigantic maze. It feels like there may be many ways in, but the way out is well hidden and difficult to reach. There are seven key turns to successfully negotiate the maze of healing.

HOW to HEAL includes:

1. **H**aving the experience. This is the entry point.

2. **O**wning the experience as a loss. This means not denying it, pretending it doesn't hurt, or minimizing its importance.

3. **W**illingness and readiness to walk the path of healing. The timing of healing is a very individual thing.

4. **H**urting. There is no quick fix and no path that allows us to avoid the pain. We must face the pain and experience it.

5. **E**xpressing and not repressing the hurt. That means finding a support system or a friend who is willing to let us experience and share our feelings. This isn't always easy. Many times our family and friends want to fix it by finding us a shortcut. There are no shortcuts to grief.

6. **A**ssessing and re-evaluating ourselves and the situation. It may seem to delay our progress, but it's a necessary part of healing. Early in grief, it feels like we'll never survive long enough to find the end of the maze. But then, somewhere down the path, we find ourselves having our first good belly laugh and feeling guilty about it. Later, we may find ourselves laughing without even thinking about it, or going the whole day without thinking about the pain. That's because we are moving into the final stages of healing and nearing the end of the maze.

7. **L**earning to live with a redefinition of self. This final step requires finding ways to reinvest our emotional energy, rather than having all of our energy stuck in re-experiencing the loss. This takes place slowly over time. Expect successes, but also setbacks and readjustments.

There is no straight line of healing from loss. In fact, there are multiple routes, including dead ends and blind spots. There are detours that cause us to change direction, often leaving us feeling lost and confused. Some of the potential detours take us through shock, denial and disbelief. Others may draw us into paths of anger, depression and despair. These dangerous detours can make us withdrawn and bitter—even destructive. If we can't find a way to turn around and reconnect with the main path, this detour is a sign of complicated grief—grief that may need special attention.

Ideally, in navigating the maze, we will learn much about ourselves. We'll leave the maze with a new depth of character—a new definition of self that prepares us to move into the future.

> *Grief and pain are the price we humans have to pay for the love and total commitment we have for another person. The more we love, the more we are hurt when we lose the object of our love. But if we are honest with ourselves, would we have it any other way?*
>
> *— C.S. Lewis*
> *A Grief Observed*

Practical suggestions

Take the little losses seriously.
By taking the time to show our caring for a friend who is moving away, or our sadness in leaving a home grown too small or large for our needs, we give ourselves an opportunity to "rehearse" for the larger losses in our lives.

Take time to feel.
Build in quiet time to be alone and undistracted. Privately writing about our experiences and observations can contribute to a sense of release and understanding.

Confide in someone.
Burdens shared are not as heavy. Accept the caring gestures and listening ears of many others graciously, recognizing that your turn to reciprocate will come.

Ritualize the loss in a personally significant way.
Find creative ways to memorialize losses—ways that fit the person you are and the transition you have undergone.

Allow yourself to change.
Losses of people and roles important to our lives change us. Embrace those changes. Find opportunities that exist for growth, however bittersweet that growth may be.

Practice your religion.
God is a great source of comfort and strength for Christians. Faith resources include prayer, Scripture and the support of your church. God and faith provide consolation and help in finding reason and purpose in life amidst the pain.

Reconnect with God's gifts.
Music, art, poetry or other ways to reconnect with some of God's gifts can help lift that cloud of despair.

Maintain a daily routine.
Consistency becomes important in relieving stress. Try to get six to eight hours of sleep a night. On the days you can't sleep, at least rest. Try to eat three meals a day. On days that food doesn't sound good, try to eat at least something.

Exercise.
It's a powerful antidote for depression. As we exercise, our bodies release endorphins. These proteins can help give us a feeling of well-being again, without the need for medication.

Release anger.
Venting anger, of course, can be done constructively or destructively. Certainly, throwing a pillow is much preferred over throwing a fist. Writing an angry letter, knowing it won't get sent, is far better than saying mean things that cause pain and perhaps regret. Find ways to vent anger constructively.

Avoid chemicals.
It's important not to try drowning out our pain with drugs or alcohol. Alcohol may seem to give temporary relief. But alcohol is a depressant, and aren't we already depressed enough? Avoid stimulants such as caffeine, nicotine and sugar. These can add to that feeling of shakiness. Generally, medications are not needed and if they are, it's for specific symptom relief. There are no pills for grief. Self-medicating can be very dangerous. It's best to consult a physician before taking any over-the-counter preparation to relieve distress. There may be times when a physician encourages use of medication. If so, follow instructions carefully and report back any changes in symptoms.

Help the body and mind work together.
Find ways to break down a task so it isn't as overwhelming as it might seem at the start. Breathe deeply. Take that walk. Watch the sunset. Go out for dinner. Sit and stare at the walls, if that's all the energy you have at the moment. Ask for help from God and from other people.

Healing takes energy. We must give ourselves time. We must resist the temptation to try to measure up to all the "shoulds" people have for us. All in all, the most important thing we can do is learn to be gentle with ourselves.

How will I know if special help is needed?

There are times when grief gets very complicated. All of the following symptoms are normal in grief. However, if they become intense and severe, causing risk to our physical, emotional or spiritual well-being, it's crucial that we get extra help.

❖ A feeling of being trapped, alone and unable to talk to family members or friends about what happened.

❖ Flashbacks, recurrent nightmares, intense anxiety and the need to tell the story over and over again.

❖ Ongoing, recurrent memories of the death or other loss that are disturbing work, home life or leisure time.

❖ A preoccupation with the loss many months after it occurred.

❖ Overidealizing the deceased.

❖ A significant decrease of interest in normal activities.

❖ Feelings of guilt as a survivor.

❖ Wishing to die, thinking about suicide, difficulty imagining a future.

❖ Violent outbursts directed at self or others, including children.

❖ Difficulty feeling happy or loved.

❖ Avoiding relationships out of fear of being left out again.

❖ Using drugs or alcohol to avoid the pain.

❖ Inability to relax because of a constant expectation that something bad is going to happen.

❖ A severe faith crisis.

> *Grief is the rope burns left behind when what we have held to most dearly is pulled out of reach, beyond our grasp.*
> — Stephen Levine

Think about the kind of help that would be most beneficial. Churches often are a good place to turn for help. Many offer professional assistance through grief ministry, prayer support and/or spiritual direction.

Whatever organization you approach for counseling, be sure to seek someone who specializes in loss and grief.

There are also peer support groups—people who have had like-situations and talk about their experiences to help you realize you're not alone. Another option would be to turn to other professional support. Help is available from therapists, psychologists or psychiatrists to explore coping strategies with you. Many professionals also facilitate therapy groups to help people explore their grief experiences together.

Whatever route is considered, it may help to have someone totally dedicated to helping meet your coping needs. Exploring your questions; validating what you're experiencing; reassuring you that you're not "losing it;" and exploring coping strategies that can help you find your path of healing.

searching for support, ask yourself:

- Would I be able to sit and talk openly in a group or do I need someone to listen to me individually?

- Do I need to hear other people who have had similar experiences?

- Am I looking for someone to help me explore my faith questions?

- Are there practical issues that I need help exploring, such as funeral rites, closing of estate, etc.?

- Do I need someone who understands medications?

- Do I need someone to help me explore physical symptoms I am having to make sure there isn't something medically wrong with me?

- Do I need someone to help me walk through the process of healing?

k potential caregivers:

- What is their level of experience—their credentials?

- Have they had any specific training in grief work? Do they work with all kinds of grief?

- How long have they been in practice? How long have they been doing this kind of work?

- Do they charge for their services? How much? Will my insurance pay for all or part of the fees?

- Ask what type of services they offer: volunteer, spiritual guidance, professional counseling, individual or group, etc.

- Have they ever had the personal experience of this kind of grief? (Know that you are perfectly within your rights asking this question, however you also need to know they may choose not to answer.)

Section II

The different faces of loss

Loss is a universal experience with many similarities and differences. This section points out some of the unique qualities of different types of losses. We'll look at what to expect during each type of loss as well as suggestions for coping.

We will explore:
DEATH, PHYSICAL LOSS, DIVORCE, JOB LOSS, POSITIVE LOSSES and SILENT LOSSES

Expected

My friends say I should consider myself lucky because I had time to say good-bye. I'm not sure that was lucky. I had to watch her suffer, day-by-day for the last four years. I watched this disease take more of her independence. There were days when I wanted to say "Stop, let's just end it all. God, please take her home." Then there were days I felt guilty for even thinking such thoughts. It was hard. I had to take over all the chores of the house. I had to learn to cook and to clean. There were days I resented her for just sitting there. Yet I knew it was a struggle for her just to breathe . She was so brave but I watched the anguish on her face. We were married 54 years. I always thought I'd die first. As I stood there watching her slip away, I was glad I was the one that got to be the caregiver. She had been such a good wife and had taken care of me for so long.

Now that she is gone, the pain is so big. How do I sleep alone in an empty bed that for 54 years had her in it, too? One night I found myself searching for her nightgown because I just wanted her in bed with me. I don't want to let go. It hurts too much. I know her suffering is over. Everybody reminds me of that. But my suffering has just begun. My friends tell me I was lucky. I don't know if I agree. Being able to say good-bye didn't take the pain away.

Is it easier when you have time to say good-bye? There have been whole books written exploring that very question, called anticipatory grieving. The consensus seems to be that even though you may have time to get used to the idea, when it's time to say that final good-bye it still hurts. There is no such thing as doing *all* your grief work before a person dies. In fact, there are some things unique to this type of death that can complicate the healing process.

One is exhaustion. It can hit one person or an entire family. Fatigue impacts the practical things that need to be done. But even more than that, it can slow the healing process because grief takes energy.

Then there is the relief experienced when death finally comes, often followed by guilt for feeling relieved. You hurt, even though you know their suffering is over.

Talk about it.

In an anticipated death, there are many things that can and should be shared. By mistakenly trying to protect each other through silence, we may deprive the warmth, the sharing and the togetherness that is so desperately needed.

Communicating can be difficult and painful. But remember that this time will not come again. Now is the time to say and do and share. With courage, this time of sorrow can be an opportunity for beautiful sharing and intimacy. If we deny each other this rich experience, there will not be another chance.

> When we lose one we love, our bitterest tears are called forth by the memory of hours when we loved not enough.
>
> — Maurice Maeterlinck
> Wisdom and Destiny

There is a void that comes with expected death. So much of your life has revolved around caregiving for the one who is dying. Where do you put that energy now? How do you fill your time?

It's easy to feel out of control in this situation. That's why it's important to focus on things we *can* control from day to day, from moment to moment. Coping in these situations requires attention to good self care, self limits and self nurturing. It also means completing the redefinition of self that began long ago; the day when the reality of an upcoming death settled in as an unwelcome visitor.

Remember, too, that prayer, faith in God's promise and the support of the community are very helpful when facing mortality. It's one of the true tests of our ability to let go and let God's will be done.

21

Sudden/Traumatic

I couldn't believe it. The knock on the door. Who would be coming to our house in the middle of the night? I opened the door and saw the police uniform. I knew something was very, very wrong. I don't think I heard anything they said except, "I'm sorry. It was a terrible accident. They're dead." I can't tell you any of the details of the accident. I don't know if they didn't tell me, or I just couldn't hear it. I was so numb. I was so angry. I wanted to hit the policeman and the chaplain that came to break the news to me. They couldn't be talking about my husband and my son. It wasn't possible. I was sure they were in their beds. I wanted to go check. They held me and they said, "I'm sorry, they're not in their beds. They never made it home."

That was almost six months ago, I still feel the pain and the numbness of that night. It still feels impossible to believe. I'm back at work, but I'm just going through the motions. I think my boss is being nice, keeping me on because I used to be a good worker.

I want someone to pay for this. It's not okay, it's not fair. How could God let this happen? Some days I just sit and cry. Will the clouds ever lift? Will the sun ever shine again?

When death—or loss of any kind—is sudden, you feel cheated. Life has given you no time to get used to the idea of having to say good-bye. An overwhelming sense of shock and disbelief settles in. *It can't be!*

It's hard to put the immediate horror to rest. We need proof. We may need to see the body even if the death was the result of serious injuries.

There is anger, pain, rage and an overall sense of unfairness. Then, for some, not having answers can lead to a major faith crisis. *How could God let this happen? Doesn't God care how much I hurt?*

The journey of coping begins with symbolically finding a way to say good-bye while coming to terms with the truth that a death has occurred. Many times, that means getting help from others. Someone who will listen to the story over and over again. Someone who might help with the details: completing the paperwork; driving past the accident scene; helping with funeral arrangements; even shielding you from the media in certain circumstances.

I am utterly crushed and groan in anguish of heart. All my longings lie open before you, O Lord; my sighing is not hidden from you.

Psalm 38: 8, 9

Just being able to put one foot in front of the other may be the hardest task you can manage in the early days following a sudden death. It's important to have friends who will help deal with your children, or meals, or even just mowing the lawn.

Another key is to find a support group of people who have had similar experiences. Here, you can find reassurance that you are not alone—that you aren't the only one who has experienced this kind of loss. Here, you are able to meet people in all stages of healing.

Finding the right support group takes time. It's not something to begin too early in grief. Usually, a good time is three to six months following a death. Don't make a judgment after the first meeting. Try two or three meetings. If it still feels too difficult, wait a few months. Remember, groups are not for everyone.

Healing following this kind of death is difficult, painful and requires lots of time and support.

Suicide

This feels like a bad dream. A true nightmare. I knew she was upset about our arguing. She told me she was in a lot of pain. She told me she wanted to end it. But I thought she meant the marriage. I never considered that she meant her life. How am I supposed to explain to the children that their mother killed herself? She not only took her own life, but she took our life together, too. And in our own home! How can we go back to the house? Can we ever again live in that house? What could she have been thinking? It's not like her. Suicide. I don't even like the word. There is no way I will be able to say that word to my friends. I think I will just need to say she died suddenly. I am angry at her. How dare she! She had no right. We could have worked this out if she had just stayed alive. I feel guilty, too. Maybe there were signs, maybe there were things I should have seen, should have done. Maybe there were ways I could have stopped her. I'll never know now.

A suicide death is one of the most difficult losses a family has to bear. With a single act, every relationship is irreparably affected. Grief is complicated by feelings of anger, guilt and shame. Everyone is left with the deafening question, WHY? Why didn't he love me enough to turn to me and talk about it? Why did she have to go to that extreme?

In a suicide, it's easy to get caught up in the "shoulds." I should have seen. I should have read the signs. I should have stopped him.

The pain for survivors is complicated. First, we mourn the loss of someone who has died. Second, we've experienced a sudden, typically unexpected traumatic death. And third, we may be shunned by a society that seems uneasy about showing its compassion following a suicide (although people generally are becoming more enlightened about it). We feel the pain of loss, yet may not know how, or where, or if we should express it.

While suicide still may carry some stigma of shame, nothing is gained by hiding it. It is a death, just as real as any other. We need to talk, cry—sometimes even to scream—in order to heal.

We need to let go of the responsibility. We need to rid ourselves of any misguided guilt. We need to accept the facts: It was *he* who killed himself. It was *she* who took her own life.

The shame and guilt of suicide may hold us back from talking about it. Yet they are exactly the reasons we need to talk. Whether it's family, friends or personal support systems, we need to get our feelings out. We need others to help us focus on the choice that was made out of the many

> *Even though I walk through the valley of the shadow of death, I will fear no evil, for you are with me; your rod and your staff, they comfort me.*
>
> — Psalm 23:4 NIV

choices that were available. Support groups are one of the best ways to do that. Call your local crisis clinic.

Other coping techniques can bring a kind of cleansing to the emotional fog that suicide brings. Writing a letter to the person who committed suicide is a way to express our pain and anger—and perhaps show our forgiveness. Or perhaps coping includes having a "conversation" in our heads with the deceased person that includes the question "why"—even if there are no concrete answers. Coping may be just standing in the shower, crying, letting all the pain run down the drain for a short while.

There may be a need to "bone up" on the subject, researching the subject of suicide as a way of personal healing. Just knowing that thousands of people commit the sad and tragic act of suicide each year can ease the feelings of isolation and abandonment. And it can let us know we are not alone.

There is, too, a special need for forgiveness and spiritual healing in these situations. We need to feel assured of the reality of God's forgiveness. If we are mad at God, we need to talk about it. Remember, having anger at God speaks of having a relationship with Him. We need to work through our anger and eventually forgive our loved one for taking a life.

These are, indeed, difficult times—times that may require the help of a skillful spiritual counselor.

This grief experience is unique. Be patient with yourself. Your life is under reconstruction.

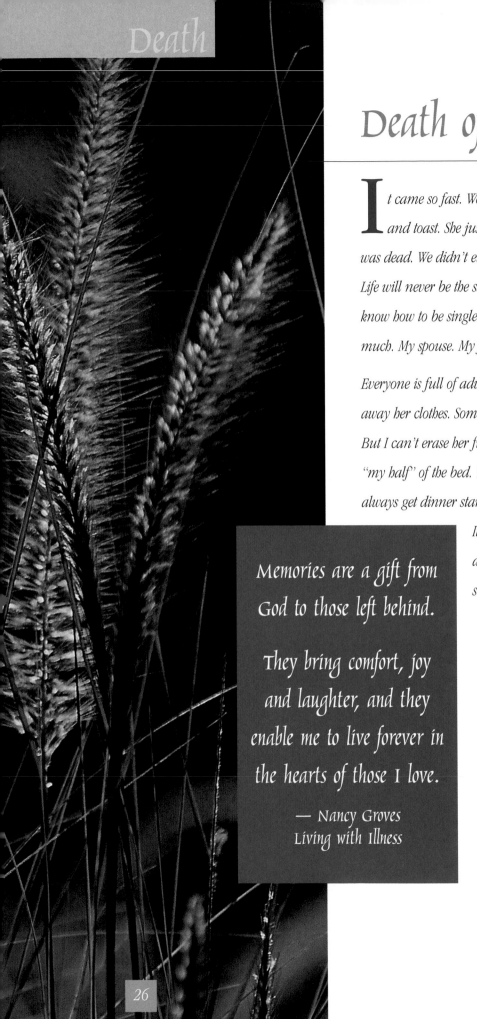

Death of a spouse

It came so fast. We were sitting at the table, talking over our coffee and toast. She just collapsed. A heart attack. Two hours later, she was dead. We didn't even have the chance to say good-bye to each other. Life will never be the same again. We'd been married so long, I don't know how to be single. I don't even know if I want to go on. I've lost so much. My spouse. My friend. My life partner.

Everyone is full of advice. They tell me to put away her pictures, to give away her clothes. Someone even said I should take off my wedding ring. But I can't erase her from my life like that. I still find myself sleeping on "my half" of the bed. The 5 o'clock hour is the hardest. For years we'd always get dinner started, sit and talk, play cards and wait for dinner. It was our time. Now, I just play solitaire. I cook and eat alone. This house is so empty now. The silence is deafening.

Memories are a gift from God to those left behind.

They bring comfort, joy and laughter, and they enable me to live forever in the hearts of those I love.

— Nancy Groves
Living with Illness

Few things are as painful as the death of a spouse. We are thrust into a new way of living that can be extremely lonely, frightening, confusing and overwhelming. It's almost as if a part of us has been taken, too. We may even wonder if there is a reason to go on.

There are tremendous psychological and physical impacts in this loss. We realize that much is lost with the death of a spouse. Gone also is our friend, lover, confidant, partner—perhaps a money-maker, cook, bookkeeper or other important role player in our lives. Everywhere we turn, another memory is triggered, another swelling of emotions is prompted.

For some people, the grief can become so severe that illness, even death, can occur within months of the loss—the result of "broken heart syndrome."

Confusion, disorganization, fear, guilt, anger and fatigue are some of the many emotions that can be expected during this time of grief. Don't be surprised if you suddenly experience surges of grief, even at the most unexpected times. They are natural responses to the death of a loved one.

As people try to be helpful, they may encourage you to clean the house and remove all the memory-makers: get rid of the clothes, clean and reorganize the cupboards, remove the photos—even suggest you remove your wedding ring. These are all activities that should be done on your schedule, not someone else's. Don't force yourself to move *your* spouse's belongings right away. Move them when you're ready.

To cope, it's important to recognize your grief as unique. No one had the same relationship you had with your spouse. No one else has your background, your experiences, your support system. As a result, you will grieve your own way. Take each day as it comes. Grieve at your own pace.

It's also important to find persons who are compassionate and who will walk with you through your grief journey. Reach out to people you can speak openly with about what you miss, what you did together, and the type of person your spouse was. Let yourself be around those who understand and support your religious beliefs. They may be caring friends. Or, they may be members of a support group who have experienced the death of their spouse.

Avoid people who try to give your grief a "quick fix" by telling you such things as "you'll get over it." Instead, your support system should include people who let you grieve your own way—and help you acknowledge your own feelings.

Certainly, memories play an important part in the grieving process. They should not be hidden or suppressed as a way to "get over" a loss. Instead, they should be treasured as a lasting legacy. If your spouse liked gardening, plant roses you know he or she would have liked. If there was a special event you shared together, create a photo album of it. Remember, there is much healing in the expression of memories.

Above all, be compassionate with yourself. Recognize what your body and mind are telling you. You may think you should be more in control of the situation. But that may only make the healing more difficult to begin.

Yes, your life has changed. But it's important to know you can survive. You can become whole again—perhaps in ways never expected—yet always remembering the one you loved.

Death

Death of a child

The first time I went to one of those support group meetings someone said, "The death of a parent is a death of the past. The death of a spouse is the death of the present. But the death of a child is a death of the future." Is that what I'm feeling—the death of the future? Future isn't even a word I recognize any more. I can't imagine the future without him. I look at other parents with their children and I want to run up to them and shout, "Love them, hold them, don't ever get angry with them, take care of them. You never know when the day will come that they won't be there anymore."

My husband and I wanted him so much. Why did his life end so soon after it began? We are really struggling. He goes to work. I just stay in this empty house. They call it depression. I call it a broken heart. I don't know if I can live without him. My friends say, "You're young, you can have another child." But that will never replace this baby. Right now, I don't want another child. I want him. Future. That woman at that meeting was right. It's very hard right now for me to imagine any future.

> ...you will be not cured, but...one day—
> an idea that will horrify you now—
> this intolerable misfortune will
> become a blessed memory of a being who
> will never again leave you.
>
> — Marcel Proust
> Letters

Children aren't supposed to die. It breaks all the rules of nature. Ever since we were kids ourselves, we were told you got old and then you died. The death of a child isn't just a test of the human spirit, but a test of any marriage, of one's faith, and of a parent's basic survival strength.

It is a death so jarring it can take years to recover—a journey that is often frightening, painful, overwhelming and sometimes very lonely. The questions, *"Why?" "How can this be?" "How could a loving God let this happen?"* are commonplace. There can be numbness, disbelief, anger and a rage that can explode at the unfairness of it all. We feel cheated; we were barely able to say hello before saying good-bye.

We question our identity as parents. After all, isn't it a parent's job to keep our children safe? Then, as if our identity isn't shaken enough, someone asks, "How many children do you have?" The truth is, there is no "right" or "wrong" answer to that question. It depends on what's comfortable for you.

Grief over the death of a child may affect a couple's relationship. Many marriages end in divorce following the death of a child. On the other hand, many marriages are strengthened by pulling together through this adversity.

It is often true that each parent will grieve very differently. Each has had a different relationship with that child—different hopes, dreams and aspirations.

Years following the death of a child, the visual image most parents hold is the age of the child when death occurred. However, most bereaved parents will continue to play the "aging game" in their head. They'll try to figure out what the child would be doing today *IF: He would have been starting school this year...getting a driver's license...picking out a tux for prom...*

Suggestions for comfort and coping

Talk about your grief.
Many times, we need to tell the story—and keep telling it, perhaps for years. We need to call on a special kind of friend. Someone who will listen—frequently and without judgment.

Share positive memories.
It may take time to get past the painful memories and get to the happy ones. But writing, talking to friends and family, or looking at old photos are ways those good memories can be stimulated.

Expect many emotions.
Don't be surprised if out of nowhere you suddenly experience surges of grief, even at the most unexpected times. Talk about them with a special friend.

Allow for numbness.
Numbness and disbelief help create insulation from the reality of the death until you are more able to tolerate what you don't believe.

Don't hurry major decisions.
Try to make decisions with your spouse or close friend. If you need time alone, let people around you know this.

Embrace your spirituality.
Express your faith, but express your grief as well. To deny your grief is to invite problems that can build up inside you.

Find positive avenues to express yourself.
It may be volunteering. It may be a new lifestyle interest. These avenues—and others—won't replace the loss, but they may help fill the void.

Ask for help.
Support groups can be helpful because people there aren't shocked by the idea of the death of a child. We can find others there who can understand the depth of the pain.

Move toward your healing.
Be patient and tolerant with yourself. It's not that you won't ever be happy again. It's simply that you won't be exactly the same as you were before your child died.

To cope, we must find our way through the dense cold fog that has descended upon our world. We must be gentle with ourselves, yet we must recognize and accept that life is not suddenly going to return to the "normal" it was before the death. Coping takes on many forms: talking, crying, constructive anger, praying and sometimes just plain holding on to whatever we can find to get us through the day.

Healing after this kind of death is hard. It takes lots of time, lots of support. But remember, there *is* hope. There *is* tomorrow. There *is* healing.

Death of a pet

We were just sitting in the house when we heard the screech of tires. We didn't even know she had gotten out and there she was lying lifeless on the ground. We took her to the vet, but there was no hope. I had no idea how I was going to explain it to the kids. It never seemed right to me to try to get a replacement dog, or tell them we had their buddy put to sleep. Maybe it will help when I tell them we tried to save her.

The first death experienced for most children is the death of a pet. Pets hold a very special place in the lives of children and the children in all of us. They are friends, confidants and good buddies. Their loss is a significant one for families, one that should not be minimized.

Each family member has made a significant emotional investment in a pet. They become part of the family. With the pet's death, that investment—that part of the family—has been taken away.

What is helpful in healing is acknowledging the loss as a loss. Allow for family discussion and the open expression of emotion. It's important to create a ritual of good-bye. That might mean burying the pet cat, dog, bird or goldfish in a special place. The ritual might include a song and a wooden marker.

It is not helpful to ignore the importance of the loss or to be embarrassed by it. Also potentially damaging is attempting to deny the importance of the pet by quickly acquiring a replacement pet. Instead, allow the death of a pet to be one of those training wheels that life provides to help us learn about grief.

Betrayed by my body

ILLNESS

So Little Left

What is it that you want, nurse?
What do you expect of me?
You want me to smile all powdered and clean.
Be pleasant, be nice and don't make a scene.
You want me to get up and eat when you say.
To follow your rules all through the day.

BUT WHAT ABOUT ME?

I try to tell you, I push you away.
You don't understand what I'm trying to say.

It doesn't much matter whatever I do.
It always ends up with me versus you.
You walk away scowling giving up in defeat,
or give me a shot that just puts me to sleep.

How can I tell you what I feel deep inside?
The words just get lost, I mumble, they hide.
My body has failed me I have little strength.
These strange surroundings make it so hard to think.

I thank you for all the care that you give.
It's so clear to me, you want me to live.
But to live is the future, I know not of that.
All that I know is right now I feel trapped.
Trapped by my body, trapped by the day,
Trapped by my God that won't take me away.

How could you have helped to relieve some of that?
It would have helped if you would have just sat.

Sat not expecting a thing in return,
not making me drink, not making me turn.
Sat just allowing me to be me,
Nasty or frightened or stubborn but free.
You see as I see it, I've lost all control.
Except for my mood so that's what I show.

© Margaret Metzgar

INJURY

What am I supposed to do now? I've been a fireman for 10 years. Now just because of one accident, they say I can't do it anymore. In truth, I knew they were right. I can't lift a ladder. I can't carry a hose. It just hurts too bad, but I never expected to be betrayed by my body. I knew I was going to be a fireman from the time I was little. I was going to be a fireman forever, and now I'm left not knowing what to do, what to be. Who am I now?

We know that the one who raised the Lord Jesus from the dead will also raise us with Jesus and present us with you in his presence. ...Therefore we do not lose heart. Though outwardly we are wasting away, yet inwardly we are being renewed day by day. For our light and momentary troubles are achieving for us an eternal glory that far outweighs them all. So we fix our eyes not on what is seen, but on what is unseen. For what is seen is temporary, but what is unseen is eternal.

2 Corinthians 4: 14, 16 - 18

AGING

I stumble on my words now. There are times I can't even remember my granddaughter's name. I never thought this would happen to me. Other people get old, but I was going to stay healthy 'till I died. Bit by bit I'm losing a part of me: my step, my wit, my iron stomach. Even crunching on a nice crisp, cold apple is hard now. I can't walk more than a block and sometimes even a block is too far. I used to believe I had the strength to do anything, but now I find myself wondering if it would just be easier to lay down and die. Then I remind myself it wouldn't just be the pain that was gone, I'd lose everything. Yet, there isn't a week that goes by that I don't have another loss to my independence.

I worry about what a burden I am to my friends, my family. They tell me I repeat my stories. They are patient with me but I know it must be hard for them, too. The family always used to look to me to fix it and make it better. I don't know how to fix this one.

It doesn't matter how we are betrayed by our bodies: illness, injury or aging. The result is the same. It is a personal insult and just like all the other losses, it forces us to redefine ourselves.

The vignettes say it best. Whether it's a temporary or permanent change, it is a change. We usually can trust our bodies to work with us rather than against us. But when they betray us, the typical first reactions are disbelief and anger.

What can hurt the most when we seem to be facing a chronic, debilitating illness is the perception of a forever downhill slide. All of the "little losses" must be recognized and grieved. But that may not be easy when what we face is "bereavement overload." That's a situation where we do not have the time or resources needed to grieve and mourn one significant loss effectively before being faced with another.

Entire families can be impacted. Whether it's helping with the caregiving, taking over financial responsibilities, or being placed in another decision-making position, families feel the results. And all we can do is sit back and watch.

We feel helpless, frustrated—sometimes without value. Our emotions, as well as our social and spiritual well-being, can be damaged.

Coping here is about finding or holding on to purpose, when it feels like it is slipping through our fingers. Coping requires faith, hope and determination. It requires good self-care and nutrition at a time when exhaustion seems to be taking up permanent residence in our world.

Challenge yourself to find a way to wake up with purpose every morning. Decide before you go to bed the one thing you are going to try to complete the next day that will give you pleasure.

If you haven't learned to ask for or accept help before, now is the time to learn.

> *I am like a penny, a very bright one. Remember, my darling children, I'll always turn up. Whenever you find a penny anywhere in the years to come, you pick it up and say, "There's Grandma!" Here's a penny, take it. It is the first of many. In time you will have a thousand reminders that I'm telling you how much you are loved.*
>
> *— Anonymous*

We used to be two

The day we got married I thought nothing would ever diminish the joy I felt in my heart. We expressed our vows, 'till death do us part. Well, he isn't dead and neither am I, but we have parted.

We used to be two, then we were three, then came the twins and that made five. We were such a happy family. I don't know what happened. I don't know where that joy went. But now it's lawyers and paperwork and trying to figure out what's best for the children.

Who gets custody of them? Do they live with him a week and then me a week? How do we handle holidays? How do we explain it to our friends—to ourselves? The hurt runs so deep. Then there is the issue of the name. He always gets to be Mr., but am I still Mrs.? Do I keep his name? Do I go back to my parents name? Do I choose a new name? And then there is money. With two incomes it was easy to raise three young children. How will either one of us do it now, on our own?

The kids feel the pain, too. They can't have all of the "in things" anymore. I almost think it would have been easier if one of us had died. Then it would just be over. This way it feels like the pain and confusion and the decision-making will go on forever.

Between 30-50 percent of the families in this country struggle with the questions surrounding divorce. They have to figure out how to make sense of their pain, their faith and the decision they have made to end their marriage. It's not easy.

How do we handle the hurt that comes with moving on, the grief of saying good-bye, the struggle to say hello to a new phase of our life?

Everyone is affected by the pain of a divorce: the parents, the children, the grandparents, even the family pets. It's not just the primary loss of a divorce, but it's all the secondary losses that go with it. Having to move, having two houses, changing your financial status, explaining the divorce to your friends, losing your friends. Another often overlooked loss for some is the sense of broken vows or failure in your promise to God.

Divorce is different from death. In death, the person is gone from this world forever. In divorce, especially if there are children, there is a lack of a finite ending. In death, there is also a ritual or a way of saying good-bye. We have a funeral. Divorce has no such ritual—no way of marking the ending publicly.

Grieving is important to the recovery process of divorce. In fact, some people say the divorce process is largely a grief process. There can be overwhelming sadness and a feeling of despair. It drains us of energy. It makes us feel helpless and lonely. Many times, it even affects us physically, especially if we find no way to express our feelings. Eating is difficult. Typically, we lose weight. Sleeping is a challenge. There may be rapid mood changes, a sense of loss of reality, depression, even suicidal feelings.

To let go of the relationship and to heal, it's important to:

Find a place to vent the unresolved feelings to someone other than your spouse or children. There is frequently a lot of anger and blame following a divorce. Coping requires finding constructive rather than destructive ways to be angry.

Decide on the right place to grieve. Set aside a time and a place to grieve (away from your work). Your emotions will be easier to control at other times.

Grieve! Cry, shout, scream—whatever you need to do that is nondestructive. If you don't, your body may express those repressed feelings in illness. Everything from headaches to ulcers.

If there are children involved, allow them to grieve. They need some sort of acceptance of their pain. Allow them to express their own feelings and emotions. Show them it's OK. Don't be afraid to grieve with them. Try to maintain as much consistency as possible. Remember, too, that children will often do everything in their power to get their parents back together.

It is a true challenge to figure out how to live your life and be yourself anew in the shadow of a former marriage. Support groups help some people.

Give yourself time to get used to your life. Don't expect that you can go from a committed married lover relationship into a successful dating relationship without taking time for your grief and redefinition. Most authors who write about divorce recognize the need for a neutral zone time—a period for you to find out who you are before establishing a new relationship.

Who am I now?

I should have seen it coming with all the downsizing that has been going on. But I thought my job was secure. I've been with the company so long. I was middle management, a good employee. How can this be happening? How will I tell my wife? My family? My friends? Where do I turn to now? How will I provide for my family? What if I can't find a job? The savings won't last forever. What if we have to move? It's so embarrassing. I don't know if I'm more shocked, hurt or angry.

Uncertainty, doubt, disbelief, confusion, shame, embarrassment, anger, fear, sometimes even relief. They are all feelings related to the loss of a job. Yet perhaps the deepest of all wounds is our loss of identity. Yes, we know we are *more* than our jobs. But because we invest so much of our time and lives into them, what we do for a living has a major impact on shaping our identity. There is a void that becomes difficult to fill.

Time can also be difficult to fill. It's hard to have extra time and no money to spend and no where to go. Then there is the waiting; not wanting to leave the house because you're waiting for a phone call or the mail.

Unemployment can take its toll on a marriage. Spouses become cheerleaders. Often, the "balance of power" changes. The spouse has to carry more of the financial burden. Arguments can erupt over anything— especially money. Emotions run high. It's difficult to find things to talk about. Occasionally, violence or destructive anger can erupt against an employer or family member out of a feeling of helplessness.

Coping with job loss requires us to redefine our goals and our self-worth. It challenges us to set timelines for what we want to do and when we expect it to be done. After all, if there's no job to go to every morning, why get up? What clothes should we put on? Where do we go to fill the time? What do we talk about at the end of the day?

Coping requires assuming tasks and completing them. Writing resumés. Mailing applications. Searching the classifieds. Scheduling interviews. We need to take charge of these responsibilities. We need to set goals for every day and rewards for reaching them.

Redefining ourselves and finding ways to reclaim our power many times can be helped by calling on our trust in God and finding strength in our faith. It's also helpful to find others we can talk to who understand, who will listen, and who won't abandon us.

> *Calamities hit saints and prophets, too...to test and try their faith, love and patience.*
>
> — Martin Luther

Silent losses

How can I get people to understand something I am struggling to understand? I made the decision not to marry when I had the chance. But that doesn't take away the pain I feel now and how my arms ache to hold the child I will never have. I wish I could make them grasp how hard it is for me to watch them carry on about their babies or tell me what a good mother I would have made. I'm tired of being an aunt to their children. I want to be a mom to my own.

In addition to all of the losses that we've already discussed, we need to acknowledge the silent losses. The hard part about these losses is that they frequently are not defined or supported as losses either by ourselves or by society.

Silent losses include such things as the loss of innocence, infertility, stillbirth, miscarriage, abortion and loss of dreams. Often, even abuse or addictions can fit into this category.

All too often the person who is experiencing this kind of loss may not understand the symptoms or may not have the support needed to cope. By acknowledging them as losses, we can define them, understand the feelings, explore coping strategies, and let the healing begin.

One of the primary difficulties with silent losses is that they are not as obvious to our general community as a death, the loss of a job, or an injury. If I have a broken leg, everyone can see it. But if we've been trying to get pregnant for over three years without success, people may just think we are waiting to start a family. Therefore, if we want the support of family and friends, we must define the loss out loud.

Other extremely painful losses that fit into this category may include a missing person, a runaway teenager or the MIAs. Those are major losses in our lives, but losses that have no definable steps that give us clues to an ending. How do you keep that loss and hope alive while at the same time continue living? How long will your support group continue listening and supporting that sense of unknowing?

Coping with all the silent losses requires finding someone to talk with whom we trust—a confidant who will share our story. It may be a friend, a support group or a therapist who will help us explore our feelings. The weight in our heart from the questions, the doubts, the whys and the guilt must be freed. In silence, that weight grows heavier and heavier.

Religious beliefs can be an important element to coping. The power of prayer is, for many, a strong and constant source of comfort during this time of grief. Prayer also is something that is learned by others during this time as a new source of peace and relief and faith to carry on. Finding a person who can serve as a spiritual guide can help a great deal. It's important not to forget during this period of sorrow that if we are willing to talk, God is always willing to listen. And respond.

Many survivors of silent losses have found that in addition to dialogue with another person, healing can be found in writing. Writing may take the form of poetry, letters or journal entries. Sharing the pain of reality with pen and paper gives it definition in a way that society doesn't.

> ...but those who hope in the Lord
> will renew their strength.
> They will soar on wings like eagles;
> they will run and not grow weary,
> they will walk and not be faint.
> —Isaiah 40:31 NIV

Positive losses

For 40 years I've had a place to go to every morning and things to do. Now I'm staying at home, retired, and having to find other ways to fill my time. It's not as easy as I thought it would be. Sure, I've looked forward to retirement. And I know it'll be a good change for me, once I get used to it. But I wish now that I'd prepared more for it. A friend of mine did plan for his retirement. Now he says he hasn't really retired, he just changed one type of career for another. He volunteers his time at the community center twice a week. I still feel kind of empty inside. What's my next job? What do I do now?

Not all things that we experience in our lives as a loss are negative or traumatic. There are things that are truly positive steps forward, but still leave us with some of the familiar symptoms of grief we've already discussed. It could be a job promotion, moving to a new city, watching your children go off to college, or joining the world of the retired. They are new experiences that hold excitement, joy and change.

It is a different kind of change. Yet any move forward requires moving from a known into the unknown and a redefinition. Another good-bye of life; another hello. A sad time; a happy time. Saying good-bye to a comfort zone we've had for a long time; saying hello to something new.

My life was suddenly divided into BEFORE and AFTER, and there was no going back to BEFORE. But then I realized I had a choice to live the AFTER. I had to decide.

— Brenda Neal

Even though these may be good and positive events in our lives, it is still change. Change that is worth acknowledging. For example, it is not uncommon to hear parents talk about the empty nest syndrome. It is a time of both pride for parents and an unexplained sense of emptiness.

As one mom put it, *"This is what I have been working for since they were born, but now that it is here, what is my next job? What do I do now? What is next after MOM?"*

No, these losses don't compare, at least in intensity, with the losses previously discussed. However, they are a type of loss. So be gentle with yourself if you experience some of the same feelings discussed earlier in this book.

Section III

Giving help to others

In the midst of the pain, shock and confusion of grief, what is appropriate to say and do? This section brings some comfort and helpful suggestions to persons who want to help others who are in grief.

Parents will also find valuable help in guiding their children through this vulnerable time.

what to say and do

What do you say to someone who is grieving? We all search for the right thing to say. We all try to help create comfort, to make things feel better. We search for that loving gesture. If only we can find the right words. Sometimes even when we plan them, saying them over and over in our head, they still don't sound right when we say them out loud. Always remember that it is better to risk saying the wrong thing than not saying anything at all.

Helping those who grieve is not always an easy task. Many times, the type of help depends on the type of loss. For example, in a divorce loss you may be asked to help a couple that is struggling with their own relationship, or children who are confused about what is happening. It's important that you not take sides, even though that's exactly what you may be asked to do.

Even in a death loss there are variations in the support that's needed. When a death has been anticipated, some of the practical items may already be done, such as the funeral arrangements, the choice of music, the choice of dress, and the choice of funeral home. Yet for those who suddenly are faced with an unexpected death, all of those practical pieces will need immediate attention.

Each loss will present itself in its own unique and individual way. Still, in each case, it's important to be sensitive and genuine. We need to remember to avoid clichés, even though it's easy to fall back on them. Instead of depending upon someone else's words, we need to let our own heart speak.

It's also important to remember timing. Numbness is a primary emotion the first few weeks of grieving. That numbness doesn't begin to wear off until four to eight

weeks later, well after most support is offered by well-meaning family and friends. Yes, we need to remember the griever during the first few weeks after a loss. But we also need to remember that person two, three, four, five and six months later.

The job of a caregiver is to honor the loss, respect the grief, recognize the pain and understand the process. It is not to "fix" it or try to take the pain away. Most importantly, the role is simply to be with the griever in their time of pain and help validate their experience. That can be done through written, verbal and practical support.

Written support

In an anticipated loss, the written support could begin before the death. Send cards, letters or notes to the family, just letting them know you are thinking about them. Following any death, send your condolences. Condolences are often hard for some people to write. The most important part is to let the writing be from your heart. If you can't find the words, send a card and add a note that just acknowledges your thoughts and prayers.

One of the other things that is always nice in written support is sending memories. After having experienced a major loss, one of the fears is:

I'm afraid I will forget them. How will I hold those memories dear to my heart?

Caregivers can help with that. If you know any of the special stories, any of the special memories, write them down. Write down how you met, or your favorite adventure. Those will become treasured keepsakes.

Written support also means remembering grievers six or eight weeks later, sending a note saying you are thinking

Suggestions for Caregivers

Be patient. Real support is never a quick fix.

Listen. Even if you've heard the story before, listen again.

Be available. Anticipate needs of the griever. Try to be there when times might be the toughest.

Offer specific help. Don't just say, "Call me if you need anything."

Don't give advice about grieving. Let the griever tell you how it is.

Don't make judgments. Don't tell bereaved people they are doing something they shouldn't, unless what they're doing is potentially harmful.

> BE SENSITIVE.
> BE AVAILABLE.
> BE QUIET.

of them. Send a Christmas card acknowledging that this Christmas must be different and they are in your prayers. If you have always sent birthday cards, send a note on the birthday of the deceased.

Many times people fear that by mentioning the name of the deceased they will create pain. That is a fallacy. Just because you are not saying the name or acknowledging the trauma doesn't mean it's been forgotten.

Verbal support

This is about getting together for a cup of coffee. It's about listening to the stories for the fifth and sixth and seventh time. It's about offering that sense of presence that says, *"I'm here, you are not alone."* It can also be about personal contact with no words being shared at all. Being a caregiver requires being comfortable sitting in silence, as well as being comfortable in filling in the words.

Most of the time support is about letting the griever know that what they are experiencing isn't strange, different or crazy. It is about normalizing the experience of grief. It's being able to say to a mother who has just miscarried, "I know this is very hard. I wish I knew what to say, but I have no magic words. I'll just sit here with you if you would like."

A supportive caregiver is all about compassion. It's knowing not to use flippant statements such as, "Oh, you're young. You can have another baby."

The person who is grieving may be angry with God for letting this terrible thing happen. Listening can be helpful therapy. You may be able to express your own confidence in the love and presence of God, even though we cannot

understand all that is happening. The words of St. Paul, Romans 15:13 are a gentle prayer you can pray for grievers:

> *"May the God of hope fill you with all joy and peace as you trust in Him, so that you may overflow with hope by the power of the Holy Spirit."*

Verbal support shouldn't stop early in the grief process. It should be offered again and again. But we also need to take the cues and clues from the griever. Some people would prefer not to talk. In those situations, we need to be willing to be with them in their silence.

Practical support

This kind of support is often the best you could provide. It's dealing with things like coffee and cookies after the funeral. It's taking care of the grocery shopping when the energy level of grievers is low. Mowing the lawn. Taking care of the kids. Going for a walk with the griever.

A widower once said that the way someone could help him the most was to help him figure out how to pay his bills. He had been married so many years and had never written a check. His wife had always taken care of them. Having someone available to help with the practicality of living is often the best gift that a caregiver can give.

Offer to do one specific task rather than asking, "Is there anything I can do?"

Special note to caregivers! Remember you are doing a wonderful service, but you won't be any good to anyone if you don't take care of yourself, too. Take time for yourself.

Do's and don'ts when reaching out to a mourner

DON'T:

Force the mourner into a role, by saying, "You're doing so well." Allow the mourner to have troubling feelings without the sense of letting you down.

Tell the mourner what he or she "should" do. At best, this reinforces the mourner's sense of incompetence, and at worst, your advice can be "off target" completely.

Say, "Call me if you need anything." Vague offers are meant to be declined, and the mourner will pick up the cue that you implicitly hope he or she won't contact you.

Delegate helping to others. Your personal presence and concern will make a difference.

Say, "I know how you feel." Each griever's experience of grief is unique. So, invite the mourner to share his or her feelings, rather than presuming that you know what the issues are for that person.

Use hackneyed consolation, by saying, "There are other fish in the sea," or "God works in mysterious ways." This only convinces the mourner that you don't care enough to understand.

Try to hurry people through grief by reminding them how long it's been or by urging that they get busy, give away the deceased possessions, etc. Grief work takes time and patience and cannot be done on a fixed schedule.

DO:

Open the door to communication. If you aren't sure what to say, ask, "How are you feeling today?" or "I've been thinking about you."

Listen 80% of the time and talk 20% of the time. Very few people take the time to listen to someone's deepest concerns. Be one of the few. Both you and the mourner are likely to learn as a result.

Offer specific help and take the initiative to call the mourner. If you also respect the survivor's privacy, your concrete assistance with the demands of daily living will be appreciated.

"Be there" for the mourner. There are few rules for helping aside from openness and caring.

Talk about your own losses and how you adapted to them. Although the mourner's coping style may be different from your own, your self-disclosure will help.

Use appropriate physical contact—like an arm around the shoulder or a hug—when words fail. Learn to be comfortable with shared silence, rather than chattering away in an attempt to cheer the person up.

Be patient with the griever's story, and allow him or her to share memories of the lost loved one. This fosters a healthy continuity as the person orients to a changed future.

Use the name of the deceased. This person played an important part in the mourner's life. It's important to recognize that by mentioning the person by name.

children grieve, too; help for parents

Who is going to take care of me?

How do they decide if you get a mommy kind or daddy kind of divorce? (Adult translation: How is the decision made if you live with mommy or daddy?)

It's okay. He'll be back, won't he?

Are you going to die? Where is dead?

Will someone take our house now that daddy isn't working?

How do you know that heaven is up and hell is down? If heaven is up, why do we bury people in the ground? When we go on the plane, will we be able to see heaven?

Is dead comfortable? Did God make her die?

Do dogs go to heaven, too?

> — Common questions or statements made by children and young adults about loss

Helping children prepare

Loss is not an experience limited to adults. Children experience loss, too. And they learn from their "little losses"—the broken toy, the torn picture, starting school, the first lost love, the death of a pet.

Children learn a lot about loss from TV, nursery rhymes and fairy tales. Unfortunately, those sources often reinforce incorrect information and fantasies about loss. A cartoon character killed in one frame is alive and ready to fight again in the next. Ghosts are shown either frightening or befriending someone depending on the script. Children are depicted as "saving the day" by somehow finding the right words to keep peace in the family.

Helping children prepare for inevitable loss experiences is an important part of parenting. It should begin long before a family is struggling through loss. The best way to start has nothing to do with loss, but instead has to do with communication. Anything we as parents can do to let our children know they can talk to us about

anything or ask us questions—no matter how silly they may sound—will help a child learn to cope.

It's important, too, that you teach your children about feelings—from joy to anger—and help them find the words to describe their experiences. We need to give them permission to express those experiences and help them find constructive ways to express their anger, without causing more pain to themselves or others. All of this is about learning to cope with loss.

The world of children's literature can also help prepare children for loss. There are many books for children where the topic of loss is gently embedded in the text. Some are included in the resource section of this book. Reading these books together with your young child is an excellent way to enter into a dialogue about coping with loss before the loss actually happens.

Following loss

Probably the most important thing to remember about going through a loss with a child is that children need simple, honest, clear answers about what is happening. They need answers that reinforce reality and dispel fantasy—especially since a child's fantasy is often far worse than the reality. And, they need answers that encourage dialogue.

Children need routine and consistency to feel secure. That means if a child's favorite meal is a banana and peanut butter sandwich, both mom and dad will need to know how to make it, after a divorce. It means an 8 o'clock bedtime applies both at mom's and dad's house.

Children wander in and out of their feelings of grief. They need to feel involved, but at the same time they need permission to be children. They need play breaks. They may also need to know that the loss is neither their fault, nor is it their job to protect their parents. And, they need to know there is always a safe adult to turn to in times of need.

Communication pointers for parents

❖ Keep answers simple, clear and honest when explaining a loss.

❖ Ask what they know and understand—and what they *want* to know. Don't assume for children or put words in their mouths.

❖ Keep the dialogue direct, avoiding clichés and euphemisms that attempt to explain away the loss.

❖ Listen to their specific words and questions, not what we may want to hear.

❖ Try to understand and accept the symbolic language of children. For example, it's common following a death for young children to "play dead" in an attempt to understand what has happened.

❖ Allow for children's feelings to surface. Sometimes that may be hard to do, especially in a divorce situation where parental anger may overshadow a child's feelings.

❖ Take time for the children. That can be a challenge when you are caught up with too much to do and not enough time to do it.

Responses to loss

Children don't grow alike. They don't learn alike or grieve alike, either. Yet there are some responses to loss that can be expected, depending on the age of the child.

Age 0 to 4

Very young children respond to such things as our emotional tension, our stress, and changes that impact their daily routine. They may be more fussy or need to be cuddled more than usual. Between ages 2 and 4, they begin to understand that something is going on, but only in relation to themselves: *"But what will happen to me?" "Who is going to take care of me?"* They are very present-oriented. Forever doesn't exist in their world. Their responses are often intense, but brief. They are sensitive to changes in their routine. Support at this age is a matter of comforting, holding, playing with and reassuring. Try to maintain regular routines.

Age 4 to 7

Children of this age begin to explore language, fantasy and magical thinking. They're also beginning to be concerned about process and are full of questions. Many times they may feel that whatever happened, it is their fault. They continue to see death as reversible and often are frightened by their fears and fantasies. This is the age where boogie men, ghosts and angels are all part of their reality.

Age 7 to 11

"Fair" is a big issue at this age and loss is never fair. In fact, it's often seen as punishment. Peers are becoming more important, so there is great concern about doing it "right" and not being different. Questions become very specific and detail-oriented. Children begin to explore the concept of forever. Death no longer is seen as reversible.

Adolescence

Everything is changing at this age. Many things seem like losses. The biggest struggle is for independence. Because of this, it is difficult for children to listen to anything adults say—especially parents. There are big attempts at thinking logically and to practice adult-like responses while still struggling with immature feelings of a young adult. There are temptations to take risks (drugs, alcohol, driving fast), especially in responding to the pain of loss.

> *Remember, any child old enough to love is old enough to mourn... With our love and attention, they will learn to understand their loss and grow to be emotionally healthy children, adolescents and adults.*
>
> — Dr. Alan Wolfelt

Help with the topic of "DEAD"

Death is an especially difficult topic for adults to explain to children. It is natural to want to protect children from death. However, those attempts often can add to a child's confusion.

In addition to the religious/philosophical explanations, it's important to explain the reality of death. This includes using the word dead, explaining what it means, as well as finding out what the child understands about the word.

Here's one approach to consider:

When we are born, God gives us a body to use for our lifetime. Our body lets us walk and play and do God's work. When we die and go to heaven to live with God, we don't need our bodies anymore.

Dead means our body doesn't work. We don't run, we don't play, we don't eat, we don't hurt, we don't breathe, and our hearts don't beat. Our bodies don't work, but all the special things we have done, all the love we have shared, all the memories we have made, go on living in the people who loved us and whom we have loved.

Don't be surprised that, as children go through different developmental stages, they often will go back and question events surrounding a death. That's normal and natural. It doesn't mean we did anything wrong when we first explained the death. This is referred to as regrieving. Adults can regrieve throughout their lifetime, too.

The following list of suggestions can help during your discussions about death with your child:

1. Stop...Breathe...Calm Yourself.

2. Think About What You Want To Say.

3. Think About How A Child May Hear Your Explanations.

4. Use The Word "Dead" And Define It.

5. Use Short Sentences And Age-Appropriate Vocabulary.

6. Do Not Promise Anything You Cannot Provide.

7. Encourage Expression Of All Feelings.

8. Listen To Their Questions.

9. Include Children In Closure Rituals.

10. Remember Grief Is A Process. It Is Not Time Limited.

© Margaret Metzgar

Holding on to hope

Holding on to hope is the challenge of all grief and loss experience. Finding the courage or energy to go on day after day requires hope of healing, hope for future. Holding on to hope is not always easy. Some days it requires all of our energy just to maintain our own lives. On other days, we at least want to believe that *for everything there is a purpose,* as we try to find the purpose in our own experience. That requires finding ways to make meaning even out of situations that may seem so meaningless. Those are the days we really struggle to find belief in the unseen.

Many people say those days of struggle are when they lean most heavily on their faith, in order to find the inspiration and comfort they need to be able to go on. After all, Scripture says,

> *"Now faith is being sure of what we hope for and certain of what we do not see."*
> —HEBREWS 11:1 NIV

There are many days, walking through that maze of healing, that require belief in God, hope and future without seeing any proof of them. Time in prayer, reading His word, and fellowship with believers can all help in the struggle of holding on.

Holding on to hope requires active participation. It is not a passive process. It requires holding on to faith in the future, at a time when we can barely survive the present. It means clinging to the belief that God is good and will help us when all that we can see seems to say that is not true.

Hope comes in small steps and we must celebrate each one of them. Hope is the first time you laugh. It is when there are enough good memories, in the course of a day, to balance the painful ones. It may be when you are finally able to find words for the poem you have been working on for months. One person shared that for her, hope was the day she was able to pay all of her bills in one sitting, instead of having that task broken up by tears. Someone else said their day of success was the first day they could walk down the cereal aisle without breaking down.

Some people find hope in becoming an activist, fighting to give purpose to the loss. That may be done by starting a support group or working with an organization like MADD, or The Compassionate Friends or an Alzheimer's support group, or any other that is specific to your loss. Maybe it will mean becoming a teacher to others, a support or comforter for someone else in their time of need.

The path is seldom clear. But somehow, some way, someday we will know that the wound is healing. We may even reach the point of offering comfort to others in need. Our faith and determination will pay off.

We will discover a new definition of self, a new depth of character.

We will find, as we stand in the sunshine of a new day, that there really is a reason to hold on to that hope.

We will realize that there is, most assuredly, *A Time to Mourn and A Time to Dance.*

Healing will continue as long as we are alive. Life does go on, not without its setbacks or its reminders, but it does go on.

I have told you these
things, so that in me
you may have peace. In
this world you will
have trouble. But take
heart! I have overcome
the world.

— John 16:33 NIV

55

Section IV

Where can you turn for help when the burden of grief is too much to carry alone?

In this section, you'll find help in identifying whom to include in your own circle of support—from family and friends to people in your congregation and community, as well as national support groups.

You'll also find a list of resources for a variety of loss situations.

Resources

The weight of grief is lighter when shared. Yet, it is very hard for many of us to ask for help. Why is it so hard? If anything, suffering with a broken heart leaves us more in need of others. Still, most of us turn first to our own personal internal support systems and coping strategies.

When that no longer feels satisfactory, we expect our families to be able to fill that need. Some families can, but more often they can't. They can't because they are grieving, too. And, as we discussed earlier, people grieve differently. That can leave us feeling abandoned, disappointed or angry. Those feelings can cause us to withdraw, or force us to expand our circle of support.

The next place we turn to for support is our friends. Friends however, frequently want to "fix" us. They want to take away our pain, and to help us return to the person we used to be. This is a very loving gesture, but understanding grief requires understanding that it can't be "fixed." It must be experienced. Friends don't always understand that side of our pain.

We need to find a supportive person or group that understands they can't "fix it," but instead will honor the experience. We need someone who is willing to accompany us on the path of healing. This may mean stretching and expanding our circle of support beyond our family and friends to the available community support. Community support may be found in a church, a pastor, peer support group, self-help group or local professionals.

> *What is most personal is most universal.*
> — Henri Nouwen

A special community support person that should definitely be included is your personal physician. We all know that stress, no matter what kind, takes a toll on our body as well as our emotions. A physician can help you monitor your physical health along this grief journey. Another professional support option is a Christian therapist or counselor who can help you monitor your mental health, as a reflection of God's great love for us.

The following pages are designed to help you list whom you would include in your own circle of support. You can create your own reference page of specific names and phone numbers to call in time of need.

The Bible also is a powerful source of support. This resource section includes selected Bible readings to comfort during various times of grief.

You'll also find a list of resources that are divided, for your convenience, into the following categories:

Chronic Illness and Anticipated Death

Sudden Death—Natural and Accidental

Death of a Child

Suicide

General Grief/Education

All addresses and phone numbers are current and accurate as of the date of printing, but as we know, all things change. If you are having difficulty locating one of these resources, or any resource, please contact your local church, crisis clinic or local telephone directory.

Personal circle of support

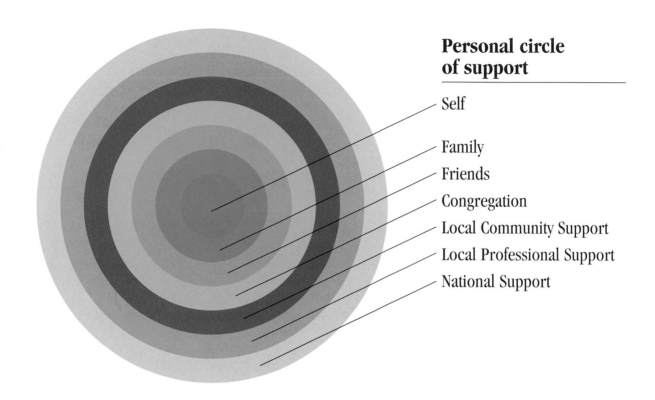

**Personal circle
of support**

Self

Family

Friends

Congregation

Local Community Support

Local Professional Support

National Support

When I need to talk to someone in my family, I can call...

(name) _____ (phone number) _____
    or
(name) _____ (phone number) _____

In my friend support circle, I can call...

(name) _____ (phone number) _____
    or
(name) _____ (phone number) _____
    or
(name) _____ (phone number) _____
    or
(name) _____ (phone number) _____

In my congregation, I can call...

(name) _____ (phone number) _____

(name) _____ (phone number) _____

(name) _____ (phone number) _____

In my local community support circle, I can call...

(Pastor) _____ (phone number) _____
    or
(Doctor) _____ (phone number) _____
    or
(Hospital) _____ (phone number) _____
    or
(Counselor) _____ (phone number) _____
    or
(Group) _____ (phone number) _____
    or
(Other) _____ (phone number) _____
    or
(Other) _____ (phone number) _____
    or
(Other) _____ (phone number) _____

National support groups I can call...

_____ (phone number) _____
    or
_____ (phone number) _____
    or
_____ (phone number) _____
    or
_____ (phone number) _____

Selected Bible readings

When angry at life or God
Psalm 22:1-21
Psalm 88

When feeling overwhelmed
Psalm 42
Psalm 86
Psalm 102
Matthew 6:25-34
Mark 4:35-41
Romans 8:31-35, 37-39
James 5:7-11

**When needing to know that
God understands loss**
John 11:33-36

God's invitation to hurting people
Matthew 11:28-30
I Peter 5:6-7
I John 3:19-20

**When in deep pain or feeling
forsaken by God**
Psalm 6
Psalm 13
Psalm 18:1-6
Psalm 121
II Corinthians 1:8-11

When needing comfort
Psalm 23
II Corinthians 1:3-7

When seeking inner peace
Philippians 4:4-9
John 14:1-7
John 14:27
Colossians 3:15

When feeling lonely
Psalm 139:1-17
Isaiah 41:10

When reflecting on death
Psalm 90

When seeking hope
Psalm 46
Psalm 130
Isaiah 25:6-8
Isaiah 35:1-10
Isaiah 61:1-3
John 11:25-26
Romans 5:1-11
Romans 8:28, 31-35, 37-39

When seeking patience
Psalm 40:1-8
Psalm 102
Psalm 118
Romans 8:18

When seeking assurance
Isaiah 26:3-4
John 10:27-30
Romans 6:3-9
I Corinthians 15:15-26
II Corinthians 12:7-10

When concerned about moving
Psalm 121:8

**When in the midst of a
bitter divorce**
Psalm 27
Psalm 64
Psalm 69
Psalm 77
Lamentations 3:55-59

**When facing a seemingly
irreversible illness**
Job 3:20-26
Psalm 143
Matthew 26:36-46
Romans 8:18-27
II Corinthians 4:13-18

**When anticipating a reunion
in heaven with those who have
gone before**
Job 19:23-27
John 14:1-6
Revelations 21:2-7

As you read your Bible, you may find other
passages that are especially comforting
or helpful to you. Use the space below to
record them for future reference.

_____

_____

_____

_____

_____

_____

_____

_____

_____

_____

_____

National support resources

Chronic Illness and Anticipated Death

American Cancer Society(ACS)
1599 Clifton Road, N.E.
Atlanta, GA 30329
(800) 227-2345
www.cancer.org
This is a national community-based voluntary health organization whose mission is to eliminate cancer as a major health problem by promoting its prevention and diminishing patients' suffering through research, education, advocacy and patient services.

The Candlelighters Childhood Cancer Foundation
3910 Warner St.
Kensington, MD 20895
(800) 366-2223
(301) 962-3520
Fax: (301) 962-3521
www.candlelighters.org
Hours: 10 a.m.-4 p.m., Eastern time
This organization educates, supports, serves and advocates for families and individuals touched by childhood cancer, empowering them to meet the challenges they face.

Make Today Count
Mid-America Cancer Center
1235 E. Cherokee St.
Springfield, MO 65804
(800) 432-2273
This is a national organization with local support groups for cancer patients as well as patients with other life-threatening illnesses.

National Multiple Sclerosis Society
733 Third Ave.
New York, NY 10017-3288
(800) FIGHT MS or (800) 344-4867
www.nmss.org
This organization supports an international program of research on the cause, cure and treatment of multiple sclerosis (MS), and has 74 local chapters across the nation to help people living with MS improve the quality of their lives. Services include information on MS, local referrals, professional and peer counseling, self-help groups, equipment assistance, employment issues and advocacy.

Alzheimer's Association
919 N. Michigan Ave., Suite 1100
Chicago, IL 60611
(800) 272-3900
www.alz.org
e-mail: info@alz.org
Hours: 8 a.m.-5 p.m. Central time, M-F, plus answering service during other hours.
A national organization that provides general information about Alzheimer's disease and can refer callers to local chapters.

Lutheran Services in America
2177 Youngman Ave.
St. Paul, MN 55116
(800) 664-3848
Fax: (651) 696-0338
www.lutheranservices.org
Lutheran Services in America is an alliance of the Evangelical Lutheran Church in America, The Lutheran Church—Missouri Synod, and their affiliated/recognized social ministry organizations.

Lutheran AIDS Network
Dr. Kristen Gebbie
Columbia School of Nursing, Center of Health Policy
630 W. 108th St., #6
New York, NY 10032
(212) 305-1794
This Pan-Lutheran association of individuals and organizations assures a Lutheran presence in response to the HIV epidemic and in support of Lutheran care, prevention and support efforts. Its primary purpose is to connect Lutherans with one another and with information resources.

National Hospice and Palliative Care Organization
1700 Diagonal Road, Suite 300
Alexandria, VA 22314
(800) 658-8898 (Hospice Helpline)
(703) 243-5900
www.nhpco.org
This organization promotes the principles of the hospice concept and program of care for the terminally ill and their families among the general public and professionals. They also provide educational programs, technical assistance and other services to meet the needs of the terminally ill and their families. Referral to a local hospice program can be made.

Sudden Death—Natural & Accidental

MADD (Mothers Against Drunk Driving)
511 E. John Carpenter Freeway, #700
Irving, TX 75062
(214) 744-MADD (for general information)
(800) GET-MADD (for victims)
www.madd.org
A national organization that provides information and materials to help stop drunk driving and to support victims of this violent crime. They can also make referrals to more than 400 local chapters.

Death of a Child

SIDS (Sudden Infant Death Syndrome Alliance)
1314 Bedford Ave., Suite 210
Baltimore, MD 21208
(410) 653-8226
(800) 221-7437 (Hotline)
www.sidsalliance.org
A national, not-for-profit, voluntary health organization dedicated to the support of SIDS families, education and research. The nationwide, 24-hour, toll-free SIDS Information and Referral Hotline listed above is available for parents who wish to talk with a SIDS counselor, request additional information about SIDS, and/or be connected to the local SIDS affiliate for support services in their area.

Alive Alone
11115 Dull Robinson Road
Van Wert, OH 45891
(419) 238-1091
e-mail: alivalon@bright.net
This nonprofit organization benefits bereaved parents whose only child (or children) are deceased. They provide a self-help network and publications to promote communication and healing. A newsletter is published bi-monthly.
An In Loving Memory Conference is held for parents with no surviving children. It is held every other year (odd years). For information, contact Glen and Linda Nielsen, 1416 Green Run Lane, Reston, VA 22090. Phone: (703) 435-0608.

The Compassionate Friends
P.O. Box 3696
Oak Brook, IL 60522-3696
(630) 990-0010
www.compassionatefriends.org
A national organization designed to assist bereaved families who have experienced the death loss of a child. Local chapters are available in most communities. Many printed resources and programs are available.

Parents of Murdered Children, Inc.
100 E. 8th St., B-41
Cincinnati, OH 45202
(513) 721-5683
(888) 818-POMC
Fax: (513) 345-4489
www.pomc.com
POMC exists to offer emotional support for survivors and contact with similarly bereaved persons, to provide information about the grief process and the criminal justice system, and to increase communication with professionals and society about the problems faced by survivors.

Suicide

American Association of Suicidology
4201 Connecticut Ave. NW, Suite 408
Washington, D.C. 20008
(202) 237-2280
Fax: (202) 237-2282
www.suicidology.org
This not-for-profit organization exists to help people understand and prevent suicide. They provide information and materials for and about suicide survivors.

General Grief/Education

ADEC (Association for Death Education and Counseling)
342 N. Main St.
W. Hartford, CT 06117-2507
(860) 586-7503
www.adec.org
This international, interdisciplinary organization is dedicated to improving the quality of death-related education and counseling. Callers can receive referrals to local ADEC member counselors. ADEC also takes an active role in educating professionals and the public in death-related issues.

AARP Widowed Persons Service
601 E St. N.W.
Washington, D.C. 20049
(202) 434-2260
www.aarp.org/griefandloss
This organization provides a wide range of information, including local support groups, educational materials and training. Calling them will result in speaking with people who are trained to talk and listen. The caller will speak with someone who has "been there." Individual counseling is not provided.

Bereavement Services
Gundersen Lutheran Medical Center
1910 South Ave.
LaCrosse, WI 54601
(608) 791-4747
(800) 362-9567, ext. 4747
www.gundluth.org/bereave
Bereavement Services promotes bereavement care across the continuum of life through a professional, interdisciplinary approach. Bereavement Services provides training programs for caregivers and support materials for caregivers and the bereaved. This resource is home of the RTS Perinatal Bereavement Program, a service for families whose babies died during pregnancy or shortly after birth.

GriefNet
http://griefnet.org
e-mail: griefnet@griefnet.org
This international resource is available on the Internet for people experiencing grief and loss. Some of the major resources available are the resource center, which includes a library and newsletter, e-mail-based support groups, memorial Web pages and others. KIDSAID, a companion Web site for children, also is online at http://kidsaid.com.

CDC National Prevention Information Network
P.O. Box 6003
Rockville, MD 20849-6003
(800) 458-5231
Fax: (888) 282-7681
www.cdcnpin.org
The CDC National Prevention Information Network is a national reference, referral and distribution service for HIV/AIDS, STD & TB-related information. Their services are designed to facilitate the sharing of information and resources among people working in HIV prevention, treatment and support services.

Bereavement Publishing, Inc.
5125 N. Union Blvd., Suite 4
Colorado Springs, CO 80918
(719) 266-0006
(888) 604-4673
www.bereavementmag.com
Bereavement magazine, started in 1987, is a support group in print. It is published bi-monthly and is designed to provide support for the bereaved. There is a yearly subscription fee.

Mourning Discoveries
Bereavement Support Services
114 Garrett's Grove
Whitesboro, NY 13492
(800) 589-3742
(315) 736-6643
Fax: (315) 736-7034
www.mourningdiscoveries.com
e-mail: mdisppt@borg.com
This consulting firm provides bereavement publications and support group referral information to families in grief.

Additional references

Grief/Coping/Losses/Death/Crisis

Beiderwieden, George. *Heaven.* Concordia Publishing House, 1967. Item # 741008.

Answers questions about heaven with texts from the Bible. Provides a comforting reassurance for bereaved families as they deal with the inevitable questions about where their loved one is.

Bockelman, Wilfred. *Finding the Right Words: Offering Care and Comfort When You Don't Know What to Say.* Augsburg, 1990.

Bozarth-Campbell, Alla. *Life Is Goodbye, Life Is Hello: Grieving Well Through All Kinds of Loss.* Hazelden Information Education, paperback, 2nd edition, 1994.

An excellent resource written by an Episcopal priest and therapist looking at all aspects of grieving and a variety of lifetime changes and losses. Easy reading, early to mid-bereavement.

Deffner, Donald L. *At the Death of a Child.* Concordia Publishing House, 1999. Item# 142029.

Addresses the emotional, physical and spiritual anguish bereaved parents experience and communicates the hope found in the Gospel. Provides encouragement and comfort. Discusses baptism in an honest, biblical manner. Includes prayers.

Faldet, Rachel and Fitton, Karen. *Our Stories of Miscarriage: Healing With Words.* Fairview Press, 1997.

A collection of 50 personal stories from those suffering miscarriages. Written to help comfort and give hope to those also experiencing loss through miscarriage.

Fitzgerald, Helen. *The Mourning Handbook: The Most Comprehensive Resource Offering Practical and Compassionate Advice on Coping With All Aspects of Death and Dying.* Fireside, paperback, 1995.

Gilbert, Richard. *Developing a Spiritual Awareness and Presence in Times of Crisis and Loss.* Connections - Spiritual Links, 1504 N. Campbell, Valparaiso, IN 46383. e-mail: rgilbert@valpo.edu

Audiocassette that explores the spiritual connections in grief, and some of the frequent stumbling blocks on that faith/grief walk. Available from R. Gilbert.

Grollman, Earl. *Living When a Loved One Has Died.* Beacon, 1997.

A timely revision of a timeless classic.

Hulme, William and Lucy. *Wrestling With Depression: A Spiritual Guide to Reclaiming Life.* Augsburg, 1995.

Writing from his own battles with depression, Hulme helps depressed persons, their families and caregivers understand depression, treatment and how people can cope. Woven into his story are his wife's struggles with her husband's illness. Her thoughts show how depression affects the whole family.

Kushner, Harold S. *When Bad Things Happen to Good People.* Avon, 1994.

Rabbi Harold Kushner was moved to write this book when he and his wife learned of their infant son's disease that promised to take his life in his early teens. This is a look at why the righteous suffer, reasons for suffering, the role of religion in our losses and our relationship with God as we struggle with our hurting.

Lewis, C.S. *A Grief Observed.* Harper & Row, paperback, 1995.

Lewis writes about how one's faith is affected by the loss of a loved one. A classic.

for those who have experienced loss and another book for those who wish to comfort others in their loss.

Miller, James E. *Winter Grief, Summer Grace: Returning to Life After a Loved One Dies.* Augsburg, 1995.
Offers relief to anyone experiencing such a loss; done through reflective text, color nature photographs and suggestions for healing activities that can help survivors cope with the grief and begin their lives again.

Saleska, E.J. *Let not Your Heart Be Troubled.* Concordia Publishing House, 1967. Item# 741001.
Prayers and Scripture texts for the bereaved. Its small size makes it convenient to carry with you.

Sims, Darcie. *Why Are the Casseroles Always Tuna? A Loving Look at the Lighter Side of Grief.* Big A & Company, rev. edition, paperback, 1992.
Available as a book and an audio cassette. An entertaining and comforting look at grief in a loving and healing way.

Smith, Harold Ivan. *On Grieving the Death of a Father.* Augsburg, 1994.
Recollections of fathers' deaths by a variety of well-known personalities.

Westberg, Granger E. *Good Grief.* Augsburg, 1976.
Expounds a healthy, Christian attitude toward grief. Encourages feeling rather than suppressing your emotions and allowing Christ to help you work through your suffering.

Lord, Janice Harris. *No Time for Good-byes: Coping with Sorrow, Anger and Injustice After a Tragic Death.* Pathfinder Publishing of California, Ventura, CA., 4th edition, 1991.

Written for those who have experienced a tragic or violent death of someone close to them, without time for good-byes. Easy reading, early to mid-bereavement.

Miller, James E. *What Will Help Me? 12 Things to Remember When You Have Suffered a Loss* and *How Can I Help? 12 Things to Do When Someone You Know Suffers a Loss.* Willowgreen Publishing, 1994.
A short book that lists practical, caring, comforting words

Children/Teens—General

Children

Boulden, Jim and Joan. *The Last Goodbye, I* and *The Last Goodbye, II.* Boulden, 1994.

Combines stories, games and various activities to help children work through a loss experience.

Giff, Patricia. *Today Was a Terrible Day.* Puffin Books, 1993.

A book and audiocassette that help us remember that just because today is bad it doesn't mean tomorrow has to be the same. Easy reading, any time, not specifically related to death. Ages pre-school to grade 3.

Guthrie, Donna. *Grandpa Doesn't Know It's Me.* Human Sciences Press Inc., New York, 1986.

A sensitive portrayal, from a child's point of view, about a family's experience with Alzheimer's disease. Ages pre-school to grade 5.

O'Toole, Donna. *Aarvy Aardvark Finds Hope.* Compassion Books, 1988. Audiocassette, 1989.

This book explores the symbolic death of a mother and brother in the animal world. The exploration of loss and grief may need the assistance of an adult to help understand the transition from animal terms to human. Picture book for all ages.

Peterson, Jeanne. *I Have a Sister, My Sister Is Deaf.* Econo-Clad Books, 1999.

A young girl describes how her deaf sister experiences everyday things. It's an excellent vehicle for explaining the world of the totally deaf and also the world of differences. Easy reading any time about one of life's losses. Ages pre-school to grade 3.

Roberts, Janice and Johnson, Joy. *Thank You for Coming to Say Goodbye.* Centering, 1994.

One of the best resources for children (and their parents) at the time of a death, and for those several days before and after the funeral.

Sanford, Doris. *How to Answer Tough Questions Kids Ask.* Thomas Nelson, 1995.

Information on everything from death and divorce to

alcoholism and AIDS. Valuable to parents who struggle with tough, sensitive issues. Includes relevant Bible verses and suggested sentences parents can use to answer children's questions.

Wolfelt, Alan. *Sarah's Journey: One Child's Experience With the Death of Her Father.* Center for Loss and Life Transition, 1992.

The child comes through ... so does the surviving parent.

Teens

Grollman, Earl. *Straight Talk About Death for Teenagers.* Beacon Press, 1993.

Helpful for teens to read. Good for their caregivers and teachers. Good for all school (and church) libraries.

Scrivani, Mark. *When Death Walks In.* Centering, 1991.

A tremendous gift to the bereaved teen who often grieves alone.

Sims, Alicia. *Am I Still a Sister?* Big A & Company, 3rd edition, paperback, 1993.

Still the best resource for children and teens dealing with sibling loss.

Helping Children and Teens Grieve

Barker, Peggy. *What Happened When Grandma Died?* Concordia Publishing House, 1989. Item# 561458.

A tender, straightforward story that helps parents explain to children what happens when God calls a loved one home to heaven.

Blackburn, Lynn. *The Class in Room 44—When a Classmate Dies.* Centering, 1991.

A story approach to helping children in an elementary class grieve.

Cassini, Kathleen and Rogers, Jacqueline. *Death and the Classroom: A Teacher's Guide to Assist Grieving Students.* Compassion Books, 1996.

An excellent resource for school personnel (and anyone else) working with bereaved children and teens.

Fitzgerald, Helen. *The Grieving Child: A Parent's Guide.* A Fireside Book. Simon & Schuster, 1992.

This book provides invaluable suggestions for dealing with a child's emotional responses and for helping a child adjust to a new life. Written by a widow and mother of four. Good reference. May be best to use when concentration is possible.

Huntley, Theresa. *Helping Children Grieve: When Someone They Love Dies.* Augsburg, 1991.

This book will help you listen to children, answer their questions and guide them in coping with their feelings when they lose someone they love. Includes help for dealing with behavior changes often accompanying a child's grief.

Jarratt, Claudia Jewett. *Helping Children Cope With Separation and Loss.* Harvard Common Press, rev. edition, 1994.

A look at the importance of helping children grieve. Many ideas for working with children and understanding how different losses affect them. Easy reading. Relates to a variety of losses.

Wolfelt, Alan. *Helping Children Cope With Grief: For Caregivers, Parents, Teachers, Counselors.* Accelerated Development, 1983.

Excellent when you need help for the children and teens in your care.

Suicide

Bolton, Iris. *My Son ... My Son: A Guide to Healing After Death, Loss or Suicide.* Bolton Press, 1995.

Available as a book or audiocassette, this will become your "best friend" on a very private and complicated journey.

Chilstrom, Corinne. *Andrew, You Died Too Soon.* Augsburg Fortress, 1993.

One of the few books that tackles the horrors following a suicide often laid upon the grieving by well-meaning religious people and religious communities.

Wrobleski, Adina. *Suicide Survivors: A Guide for Those Left Behind.* SAVE, 2nd edition, paperback, 1994.

One of several books by this author that quickly cuts to the heart of the uniqueness of post-suicide grief.

Parents, Children and Divorce

Gardner, Richard. *The Parents Book About Divorce.* Bantam, revised and updated, 1991.

A comprehensive book for parents. Explains how to tell children about divorce and expected reactions, how to help in the adjustment process, and other practical details.

Reed, Bobbie. *Life After Divorce: How to Grow Through a Divorce.* Concordia Publishing House, 1993. Item # 123199.

A practical handbook for growth through each stage of recovery from divorce. Includes activities to promote healing, such as journal-keeping, reflection questions and daily affirmation. Addresses practical concerns to help you, your children and your relationships.

Smoke, Jim. *Growing Through Divorce.* Harvest House, 1995.

Written by a pastor with concern for the Christian going through a divorce.

Children's Books on Divorce

Brown, Laurene and Brown, Marc. *Dinosaurs Divorce: A Guide for Changing Families.* Little, Brown & Co., 1988.

Features cartoon dinosaurs coping with all the real issues of divorce. Ages pre-school to grade 3.

Krementz, Jill. *How It Feels When Parents Divorce.* Econo-Clad Books, 1999.

Children ages 8-16 share their stories of divorce. Grade 5 and up.

For Those Who Help

Biebel, David. *How to Help a Heartbroken Friend: What to Do and What to Say When a Friend Is Going Through Tough Times.* Baker Book House, 1995.

A guide to loving and befriending someone in a personal crisis: grief of approaching death, loss through death or divorce, serious illness or other trauma.

Childs-Gowell, Elaine. *Good Grief Rituals: Tools for Healing: A Healing Companion.* Station Hill Press, 1992.

This small, practical book explores a variety of rituals all designed to promote healing from grief.

Limbo, Rana and Wheeler, Sara. *When A Baby Dies: A Handbook for Healing and Helping.* LaCrosse, WI: Lutheran Hospital—LaCrosse, Inc., paperback, 1998.

This publication is for families and professionals. Includes miscarriage, ectopic pregnancy, stillbirth, newborn death and loss in a multiple gestation pregnancy.

Manning, Doug. *Comforting Those Who Grieve, A Guide for Helping Others.* Diane Publishing Co., 1999.

A compassionate guide for ministers, counselors, family and friends. It provides practical, caring ways to help those in mourning cope with their loss. Easy reading.

Zunin, Leonard and Zunin, Hilary. *The Art of Condolence: What to Write, What to Say, What to Do at a Time of Loss.* Harper Perennial Library, 1992.

This is a "must" book for those who help. It is a practical guide for responding following a loss. Easy reading.

Lutheran Publishing Houses

(ELCA)
Augsburg Fortress Publishers
P.O. Box 1209
Minneapolis, MN 55440-1209
(800) 328-4648
(Customer Service)
(800) 426-0115
(Corporate Office)
(612) 330-3455 (Fax)
(800) 722-7766 (Fax)

(LCMS)
Concordia Publishing House
3558 S. Jefferson Ave.
St. Louis, MO 63118-3968
(800) 325-3040
(314) 268-1111 (Local)
Note: Specific ministry phone
numbers are available from their
catalog.

(WELS)
Northwestern Publishing House
1250 N. 113th St.
Milwaukee, WI 53226-3284
(800) 662-6022 (For orders)
(800) 662-6093 (Customer Service)
(414) 475-6600 (Local)

Other Resources

(call or write for catalogs or additional information)
Transition and Loss Center
15032 37th N.E.
Lakeforest Park, WA 98155
(206) 367-4880
Consulting, speaking, training.

World Pastoral Care Center
PMB #338
1030 Summit St.
Elgin, IL 60102
(847) 429-2110
Resources, programs, consultation.

Willowgreen Productions (effective July 1, 2000)
10351 Dawson Creek Blvd., Suite B
Ft. Wayne, IN 46825
(219) 490-2222
Audiovisual productions and presentations related to loss
and grief.

Centering Corporation
1531 N. Saddle Creek
Omaha, NE 68104
(402) 553-1200

About the author

Margaret Metzgar, M.A., CMHC, is the founder and primary therapist at the Transition and Loss Center in Seattle, Washington. She specializes in working with individuals, families, children and groups dealing with issues of crisis, loss and transition. Ms. Metzgar has been doing crisis intervention and counseling since the 1970s. In addition to her private practice, she conducts professional training and workshops, and is a noted national and international speaker and published author.

Other contributors:

❖ Robert A. Neimeyer, Ph.D., Department of Psychology, University of Memphis

❖ *Bereavement* Magazine, Colorado Springs, Colorado

Photography:

❖ Dr. James E. Miller, Willowgreen Productions

❖ Dave Kaphingst, AAL, front cover and page 13